Deliciously Wheat, *Gluten* & Dairy *Free*

Antoinette Savill

Grub Street | London

For Richard, with love

Published in 2015 by
Grub Street
4 Rainham Close
London
SW11 6SS

Email: food@grubstreet.co.uk
Web: www.grubstreet.co.uk
Twitter: @grub_street
Facebook: Grub Street Publishing

Copyright this edition © Grub Street 2015
Text copyright © Antoinette Savill 2015
Designed by Sarah Baldwin
Photography by Regula Ysewijn
Food styling by Jayne Cross

A CIP catalogue record for this book is available from the
British Library.

ISBN 978-1-910690-11-6

Printed and bound by Finidr, Czech Republic

Contents

Introduction

Cooking and baking is everything to me, it is both focusing and grounding. When I feel tired, it revives me and I get energized. If life throws a wobbly then I gravitate to my kitchen where I can regain calm by browsing through recipes and bake a new cake or wicked dessert. Weighing, chopping, mixing and tasting takes time and becomes absorbing and comforting. The joy of making something special for those you love is fulfilling and satisfying and meets the need to give and share. My kitchen is large and bright, full of sunshine and a feeling of fun which is no doubt why friends and family love to perch around the huge table and devour everything on offer. Writing a cookbook is to me, immensely exciting and I am never daunted by the thought of developing another 100 or so recipes. It is for me, a voyage of discovery and learning which I feel is the whole point of life. I hope you will enjoy these recipes, some of which are tinged with Australasia, with ideas from my new home on a farm in New Zealand. There are so many fabulous new and fresh ingredients for me to experiment with here. The enormous variety of gluten-free products that are available in Christchurch, have widened my breadth of vision and been a total joy to work with.

Deliciously Wheat, Gluten & Dairy Free is about eating the right things and thinking about what is best for us health-wise and time-wise. Simple homely comforts are always needed but treats and indulgences can also have a place in our weekly menus. I think that our well-being can so easily be put back onto an even keel with the right balance of foods. The time spent on cooking and the time spent on enjoying it is vital to our bodies and our well-being. Not only at home but at work there is also a need to consider the way that we live, how we shop and eat with or without a food intolerance. Think about food as nourishment with pleasure and not just fuel so that we can work or study. Avoiding the all too easy route of junk or convenience food which is high in salt, sugar and additives or preservatives. There are recipes here that can easily be taken to work or the place of study which will be satisfying on all counts. I often think that food has its own language to us and that if we listen to it, we can take better care of our body and mind. I have heard endless times from both adults and children of all ages that they don't like certain foods and so they consciously and unconsciously avoid them. I think if we all did this much more often that we would all feel a lot happier and healthier. At the moment added sugar is the demon of the fashionable foodies. Excluded by many to the extent that they eat only sugar-free and raw food desserts and snacks, which is all very well some of the time but fills me with dismay as a permanent way of living. I do think that the old saying of 'a little bit of what you fancy' is the happiest and healthiest route through life. So, this book is also about special treats as they can be a well-earned pleasure and through life we need to be encouraged by small doses of life's exquisite things. By this, I of course mean gastronomical delights and yummy sweet things. I have reduced the sugar content in my recipes wherever possible and used honey and maple syrup as a healthier option.

Eating food and drinking wine whether on your own, with a partner, friends, family or business associates doesn't need to be ostentatious or showing off to be a little taste of heaven. Just a brief experience of pleasure can lift us for the rest of the day. Food changes our mood as well as keeping us healthy whether we have food allergies or intolerances or just wish to be living to our full potential health-wise. I feel that it is well worth the time that it takes to source good local and seasonal ingredients and to prepare the food with care and pleasure whatever diet we are following. Food is a common language between all people and everyone should be able to eat what is good for their body, what gives them pleasure, for the people who grow it and for the planet, even with special diets and food restrictions. I am not saying that one has to be a saint about it all but that if we can choose recipes that are in season or buy locally-sourced products then we have the bonus of the feel-good factor as well as the do-good factor. We are often estranged from the natural processes by which food is grown and produced and I wish that schools would take this on board and

teach our young so that they can ensure that even though some of us have dietary limitations, we should take care of what we eat. In the course of our busy daily lives, how often do we let ourselves relish the act of preparing and eating food?

Our frenetic pace of life means that our meals often fall victim to time, care and appreciation. The steady march of packaged, artificial and unhealthy fast food not only affects our well-being but particularly that of our children. This is why my faster food recipes bear good health in mind as well as being speedy, losing none of the care or pleasure of the preparation or cooking. It's neither instant food nor is it junk food, but food which is suitable for people who enjoy cooking but do not have the time for lengthy prep and cooking. It doesn't matter how busy you are, you still need to eat and so I hope that these recipes will fit into all sorts of busy schedules and lifestyles.

Even if you live in a town or city it is often easy enough to get to the countryside and such a joy to go for a walk in the woods or fields to forage for wild ingredients. We go out with the children, and think it is great fun to put on rubber gloves and pick the nettles or wild garlic leaves, seeing who can pick the most without being stung! Wild ingredients when foraged for, picked off the hedgerows or gathered from pick-your-own fruit farms, are fresh and nutritious. They need to be prepared and cooked on the same day not a few days later when you have a bit of time. This is another reason for making the recipes easy and as fast to prepare as possible.

Careful prep of food does not mean that you are going to be slaving away for hours; sometimes it means that the ingredients take time and care to be picked or collected, and other times it means that one part of the recipe needs long, slow cooking, marinating or freezing but you need not be around all the time and can be getting on with other chores or preparations for your meal or party. Although I love cooking I have always tried to shorten and simplify recipes to make them do-able in the given time between school runs, work and play. If a recipe is too complicated and too long then most of us will be put off even attempting it which would be a great pity.

Over the boom and the bust years of shopping and food preparation, in general, quantity replaced quality and we filled our trolleys to the brim with all the tempting new products that the superstores offered us. The special offers, the two for one product that we just had to have because it was a bargain, but which in fact wasted away collecting mould at the back of the fridge, or lay in centimetres of ice in the deep-freeze. When there is so much of something it no longer captures the spirit or experience of being special. If every shelf is brimming to overflow with every imaginable product we lose the fun of sourcing harder to find or more interesting ingredients. It does of course make life simpler and easier and makes cooking faster and more time-efficient, but it loses the challenge and pleasure that for example a stroll through a farmers' market or local wine merchants can give. With excess of any description we often lose the capacity to savour things properly. Over-indulge and the novelty quickly wears off, things eventually taste stale and no longer excite us but reduce the quantity and we can restore our ability to enjoy everything. So, this is why I have built up a new collection of special treats to be enjoyed occasionally and not on a daily basis.

To me this means returning to seasonal, local and sustainable foods wherever possible and I have tried to adhere to this throughout the book. This means using the national and local expertise accumulated over generations and so nearly lost in the mass production of everything. Returning to the unique expertise each area of the country has and buying foods that have the minimum of air miles that are beneficial to the community that grows or rears the products, is paramount to me. All countries worry about 'food security' (ensuring that everyone has enough food to eat) but since the global depression lots of countries are considering 'food self-sufficiency' (growing it yourself) as a more important goal. Climate change may affect what we grow in the future and how self sufficient countries can be. This is where the Slow Food movement is such a boon to countries all over the world, as it helps us to understand how important both food security and food self-sufficiency is. Even though I no longer grow my own soft fruits and cannot grow any vegetables in my very windy garden in New Zealand I am lucky enough to be able to get everything I want locally and to grow my own herbs in pots on the sheltered veranda. However, I now have our farm lamb, pork, beef in abundance and some venison and duck occasionally. It is an extraordinary thing to be able to pick some grapefruits and make marmalade within a few hours or pick lemons in the sunshine and make lemon curd or a lemon drizzle cake. Picking avocados or kiwi fruit is still an astonishing pleasure for me and the source of much creative and culinary fun.

Luckily, in England, we have the luxury of reasonably predictable weather that is good for farming and growing our own foods. We are secure in the knowledge that extreme weather conditions do not destroy our harvests or animals time and time again. We have the pleasure of a constant supply of food and drink, so I really feel that we should take a much clearer look at what we are consuming and how it is produced and delivered to our table. We all desire comfort, pleasure and sustenance and I hope that in this cookbook I can conjure up a collection of recipes and ideas that will harmonize all these requirements and at the same time give you an occasional whiff of luxury and moments of pure magic and yet still be wheat, gluten or dairy-free.

I came across a selection of slow cook recipes not long ago, which sounded delicious, cheap and easy but took a very long time to cook. I am a passionate cook and love trying out new recipes and enjoy every minute of cooking but I thought that endless slow recipes would be the most hopeless use of very precious time. So, I reckoned it would be smart to think of a way of balancing the enjoyment of cooking and eating these recipes by allowing for the express cooking that we need in our hectic times. So, this collection of recipes is a selection of slow and quick recipes to mix and match in a way that suits you. The slower recipes don't really take that long to cook or to prepare but at some point there is a waiting game. Ice cream for example has to be churned and frozen. Certain components of the recipe may take time to cook or to cool before the next step can be taken or the finished product is ready. So, don't be put off by a slower recipe because it may just be that it has to rest or mature. None of the recipes take ages to prepare or to cook, that simply is not my style! You may not agree with some of my divisions but it only a helpful guide so please do take it is in the spirit it has been done. They are marked Ⓢ for slower and Ⓠ for quicker.

I have picked as many new recipes as I can that are wheat, gluten or dairy-free as a matter of course and I have created delicious recipes to reflect up-to-the-minute tastes around the world. Naturally, I hope that you will experiment with them and re-create them to suit you whether you change them to gluten- and dairy-free or wheat-free and lactose-free for example. Play around with them and make them work for you and your friends and family. It is such a strange new world when you are suddenly diagnosed as a coeliac or as intolerant to wheat or dairy. I have plenty of helpful information to guide you through the restrictions and suitable ingredients and also a lot of advice of how life can be made easier and more pleasurable within the parameters of the dietary restrictions.

For this book, I have made up a new, reliable and delicious plain gluten-free flour mix (see page 180) which produces perfect baking and sauces every time. I have constantly used this mix with all recipes. The texture, colour and versatility of the mix has been astounding and improved the end results dramatically from using many of the branded ready-made flour mixes. Having said that of course, I have also tested every recipe with a branded ready-made gluten-free flour mix with great success. After years of trying just about every allergy-free product on the UK market I have selected and used only the best products and alternatives but flours vary enormously; different flours have different textures, varying absorbency levels and slightly different tastes which can make a vital difference in how the recipe turns out. You may have to accommodate any difference in flour varieties by working out whether it needs a bit more liquid or a bit less or a fraction more of a rising agent or a fraction less.

Throughout the book I have tried to source the most natural ingredients that I can, but this is not always possible as the ingredients need to be easy to find in supermarkets, shops and markets. I hope that you will enjoy the recipes in the spirit that they have been created.

My advice when you are choosing recipes from any book is to make sure that you balance your time to suit your lifestyle. Those who love food often luxuriate in dreams of creating a hedonistic feast for a special occasion and are in culinary state of euphoria while gazing with delight at a new cookbook. It is a wonderful feeling but usually means you are so busy that you don't have time to enjoy yourself and communicate with those you love or have fun with. It is tempting to try and magic up a dinner of three time-consuming recipes but unless you have all day to do this, it is not a good idea and you end up not really enjoying the experience. My preferred choice is to have the time to cook some of the food the day before which I can then heat up. This then gives me time to enjoy making some inspiring dishes the next day. I would have to admit to being exceptionally organized, I plan a weekend of house guests or even just a supper after a book club discussion with the girls like a military campaign. I choose my menu and plan how minimal I can make the last-minute preparations. It is no fun whizzing backwards and forwards to the oven or hob, while everyone else is gossiping and sipping the wine! I like to be very relaxed when entertaining and not stressed that something is over-cooking or under-performing.

My website and email address are listed in this book and I hope that you will let me know if I can help you in any way with the recipes.

I hope you will be as passionate about this new collection of recipes as I am and enjoy and savour every recipe that you try.

Helpful Hints and Information for a Gluten-Free Diet

As you will know, if you have coeliac disease, then the only treatment for this condition is to be on a gluten-free diet. This is such a learning-process at the beginning and the consequences of eating gluten vary enormously. Some people end up in hospital and some have mild repercussions. Either way, eating gluten damages your gut if you eat it by mistake so it is worth sticking to the diet however your body reacts. I am here to help you to enjoy your diet and revised way of life with this new collection of recipes so delicious that you will forget that you are gluten-free. Everyone else can enjoy them too and that is why these recipes were created.

Making the occasional mistake and eating gluten from time to time will not cause lasting gut damage which is a relief. Symptoms usually start within a few hours of eating the culprit food and can last several hours or days which can be very worrying. But my advice is to get right back on track and the effects should calm down and you will feel more comfortable and write a mental note to yourself never to eat that product again! The effects vary from person to person, depending on how much gluten you have eaten. So, a whole pizza is not really a good idea whereas a dash of soy sauce might not be so drastic. It also depends on how long you have been on a gluten-free diet. When recently diagnosed it is easy to make a mistake but don't berate yourself and help is always at hand with coeliac advice helplines or your doctor.

The time it takes to feel better on a gluten-free diet varies enormously. Many people feel improvement within a few days and usually symptoms like nausea, diarrhoea and bloating clear up within a few weeks. Some symptoms take longer to improve and sometimes one symptom improves and another doesn't. Generally it takes the gut damage about six months to two years to heal, so this is where creativity and variety in the food you eat is helpful with the time issues.

It is not just food that you have to be wary of but drinks too. There are a few alcoholic and soft drinks that should not be imbibed. Avoiding grain-based spirits like whisky and soft drinks made from barley such as lemon barley water is essential as is abstinence from all beer, lager, stout and ales. Luckily, there are some delicious alternatives now and they are readily available at all good supermarkets or good health food stores.

The good news is that there is plenty you can eat and drink. Cider, Perry and wines from all over the world are fine. Sherry, port, spirits and liqueurs are fine too, so they are all good ingredients to cook with in order to enhance flavours and create depth and interest to your dishes.

All the big allergy and coeliac society websites have lists of suitable foods and food products which are totally safe for you and this is very helpful to have at hand until you know your way around the diet. There are plenty of gluten-free substitute foods on the market now and you are spoilt for choice. Almost everything can be re-created without gluten once you have tracked down some good substitutes and very good recipes.

The gluten-free breads are now pretty good as the big commercial bakers have decided to produce seeded loaves and loaves with interesting ingredients such as olives or nuts. They will never be as delicious as whole wheat or rye breads but they are fine and a great treat to be able to have something simple like scrambled eggs on toast without dreading eating the toast.

Some ingredients are confusing as they can be made from wheat but the final ingredient is gluten-free, for example glucose-syrup. So my advice is always to read the label on everything you buy unless it is naturally gluten-free.

Naturally gluten-free products mean items such as seafood, vegetables, fruit, poultry, game, meat, pulses and rice. If you buy them in their natural state and you cook it, not only is it safe but you can end up healthier as you are not eating processed foods or foods that have had ingredients added to them to enhance their flavour or texture. Occasionally, we all have to have some fast food and this is particularly difficult when on a gluten-free diet. When I and my family are travelling around the world or the UK, we generally stick to a big bowl of chips for lunch if there is nothing suitable or fast enough. If the cafe or bar makes their own mayonnaise then that is delicious. In the Far East it is easy to have a bowl of rice noodles and sesame oil. The best advice is to think about how much fun you can make the food you eat anywhere in the world even if it is simple but different and fresh. That is all it takes for a holiday to be a positive experience. I find it is best not to ask for complicated dishes to be gluten-free unless the menu already says so and even then I do double-check the ingredients with the chef before ordering. Sometimes chefs are not that sure what is gluten-free and what is not. So do be wary of menus! There is a list of restaurants that you can safely go to in your country and this should be available on your Coeliac Society website.

The Food and Drink Directory lists around 15,000 foods which can be eaten even though they are processed, such as ready-meals, soups, pasta and pizza dishes and breakfast cereals etc. Keep a copy in your bag and then if you have an impulse to shop you are safe and don't end up wasting money on a product that you later find that you cannot eat.

If you are on prescription foods from your doctor you will be able to get some of these from your pharmacy but in general you have to find out where the best outlets are in your area or benefit from ordering on the internet. Variety is what I council and that is why I keep on writing cookbooks to tempt your taste buds.

A lot of people who choose not to eat wheat as it disagrees with them find that they can tolerate small doses of wheat such as in soy sauce or Worcestershire sauce. This does make life so very much easier for everyone and even easier if you are lucky enough to be able to tolerate spelt or some of the other ancient wheat grains. This opens up an avenue of products such as breads, baked products and cereals. If you can tolerate yeast then that is also very helpful and widens the repertoire of foods. As many people who cannot tolerate gluten or wheat don't tolerate yeast, I have made all my breads yeast-free in this cookbook. They are all soda breads but the up-side is that they are quick and easy to make.

My advice for anyone starting out on the gluten-free or wheat-free road is to ensure that you always have snacks in the car, in the fridge and store cupboard and in your bag or luggage. A little box or packet of dried fruit or nuts or a mixture of the two, packet of biscuits or cookies and a mini-bar of dark chocolate can prevent a drama when suddenly stranded somewhere without gluten-free snacks.

I wish you the best of times using this cookbook and I hope that it gives you many years of pleasurable and safe meals, snacks and treats.

Antoinette Savill

Soups, *Starters,*
Snacks, Lunches
& Suppers

Only pick very young nettles so that you leave the older and larger leaves for the caterpillars and egg-laying butterflies. It is wise to wear long thick rubber or leather gloves but if you do get stung the natural remedy is usually close at hand. The dock leaves contain chemicals for neutralizing the sting and cooling the skin. I am happy to say that neither my daughter nor I have been stung when foraging for this zingy soup. Use watercress and spinach leaves instead, if nettles are unavailable.

Zingy Cream of Nettle Soup

Serves 8
Wheat, gluten and can be dairy-free

450g/1lb potatoes, peeled and quartered

55g/2oz lactose-free/ goat's butter or dairy-free sunflower spread

1 very large leek, trimmed and sliced

2 large onions, peeled and chopped

150–200g/5–7oz young nettle tops with young stalks, washed and roughly chopped or watercress and spinach leaves mixed for an alternative soup

2 litres/3½ pints home-made or instant vegetable or chicken stock/bouillon (check labels for allergens).

Sea salt and freshly ground black pepper

Freshly grated nutmeg to taste

4 tablespoons lactose-free cream/goat's double cream or dairy-free soya single cream

Optional: Fresh chives or parsley, chopped for decoration

Cook the potatoes in a pan of boiling water until nearly soft, drain them and set aside. In a large thick-based pan, melt the butter or spread and stir in the leeks and onions. Cook gently until softened but not browned.

Stir in the potatoes and then the nettles. Add the stock/ bouillon and bring the soup to the boil.

Simmer the soup for about 20 minutes, leave to cool and then blend the soup in a liquidizer until smooth. Return the soup to the pan and season to taste with salt, pepper and nutmeg. Reheat the soup gently and then serve the soup in warm bowls with a swirl of cream. A few snips of chopped chives or parsley for decoration if you like but it is delicious as it is.

Wild garlic has a more subtle and milder flavour than cultivated bulb garlic. This soup becomes a perfect spring and summer dinner party starter with a swirl of cream and one or two white wild garlic flowers floating in it. The flowers are edible as well as pretty. Wild garlic has been used for thousands of years to maintain and improve health but faded in use when bulb garlic became an agricultural crop.

Cream of *Wild Garlic* & Potato Soup

Serves 6–8
Wheat, gluten and
can be dairy-free

2 tablespoons olive oil

2 medium onions, chopped

2 medium leeks, trimmed
and sliced

750g/1lb 11oz potatoes, peeled
and roughly chopped

2 litres/9 cups home-made or
instant vegetable or chicken
stock/bouillon (check label
for allergens)

255g/9oz fresh, wild garlic
leaves

Sea salt and freshly ground
black pepper

A swirl of lactose-free/goat's
cream or dairy-free soya
cream per person

Optional: Wild garlic flower
heads for decoration

Heat the oil in a large thick-based pan over moderate heat and add the onion, leeks and potatoes. Cook until slightly softened but do not brown. Pour in the stock/bouillon and continue to cook the vegetables until the potatoes are soft. Add the wild garlic leaves and cook for 5 minutes, add plenty of seasoning and leave the soup to cool.

Purée the soup until smooth and transfer back to the pan. Reheat the soup just before serving, it should be very hot but do not boil. Swirl some cream into each bowl of soup and decorate with some flowers.

This is such a quick and fun way of using up windfall apples of any kind, even bruised ones. Simply cut out the damaged bits of apple and weigh the good apples.

A bit more or a bit less won't make much difference but I do recommend only using white onions as red onions will give a strange colour to the soup. This soup is delicious when served with any of the soda bread recipes on pages 165–166.

Cream of Onion, Apple & Cider Soup

Serves 6
Wheat, gluten and can be dairy-free

115g/4oz lactose-free /goat's butter or dairy-free sunflower spread

1kg/2lb 2oz large white onions, peeled and very finely sliced

3 cloves garlic, chopped

1 large bay leaf

2 large, tart apples, peeled and core removed

750ml/3 cups home-made or instant vegetable or chicken stock/bouillon (check label for allergens)

Fine sea salt and freshly ground black pepper

330ml/1⅓ cups local cider

500ml/2 cups lactose-free/ goat's/sheep's milk or dairy-free almond & coconut milk or unsweetened soya milk

Chopped fresh chives to serve

Melt the butter or spread in a large pan with a thick base, over medium heat and sweat the onions until soft with the garlic and bay leaf.

Meanwhile, slice the apples finely and then combine with the onions. Pour over the stock or bouillon, season and cook gently for about 10 minutes. Add the cider and milk and cook for about 20 minutes. Remove the bay leaf.

Cool the soup to blend in a liquidizer. Season to taste and reheat until hot and ready to serve. Sprinkle with chopped chives.

This is my favourite American dip and I use it as a hot dip with drinks or at a barbecue. It is also my impromptu starter for unexpected meals when our guests stay on and need feeding fast! I always have the ingredients in my store cupboard and refrigerator.

Hot Artichoke *Dip*

Serves 6 as a starter
Wheat, gluten and
can be dairy-free

1 clove of garlic, minced

1 tablespoon finely grated red onion (or any sweet variety)

250ml/1cup of mayonnaise (check labels for allergens)

Good pinch of cayenne or smoked paprika powder

2 heaped tablespoons of grated Pecorino sheep's cheese or a hard goat's cheese. Dairy-free grated Parmezano or other brands or lactose-free hard cheese, finely grated

Fine sea salt and freshly ground black pepper

390g/14oz can artichoke hearts, drained and rinsed

Blend the first five ingredients. Season with salt and pepper. Drain the artichokes, chop into small pieces and stir into the mayonnaise mixture. Transfer the mixture into an oven-proof serving dish, bake in the oven for about 15 minutes or until bubbling and golden.

Serve warm with any allergy-free style dippers such as corn chips, rice crackers, carrot sticks or fingers of gluten-free pitta bread.

Please note that the mixture will separate if you put more cheese in the dip.

1 tablespoon olive oil

1 chopped chilli, deseeded if you like it milder or a pinch of dried chilli flakes

1 large clove garlic, chopped

1 teaspoon ground cumin

1 teaspoon cumin seeds

750g/1lb 11oz cooked beetroot/beets, (keep the stems on and boil them until tender in water or bake them with some oil, wrapped in baking foil) or buy them ready prepared (3 packs and no vinegar) and boil them in water for a few minutes to heat them through.

Fine sea salt and freshly ground black pepper

Juice of 1 lime or more if necessary

2 teaspoons of horseradish sauce (check label for allergens) or use freshly grated horseradish mixed with lactose-free cream, whipped, whipped double goat's cream or dairy-free soya whipped cream

3-5 tablespoons of plain set Greek-style lactose-free/goat's/sheep's yogurt or a soya cream cheese style spread or dip – all at room temperature

4 gluten-free pitta breads or make the Speedy Seeded Flatbreads recipe on page 167

Plus enough olive oil, chopped fresh chilli or dried chilli flakes and crushed garlic mixed together in a bowl to brush over the pitta breads.

Common red beetroot or beet was introduced in the 17th century to Britain and was a popular salad but then gradually by the 20th century was dwindling in popularity and it was massacred by malt vinegar and packaged in plastic. It became an underrated vegetable and in general most people didn't know about or grow any of the other gorgeous varieties which can be golden or even stripy. Now however, the hippest restaurants have diverse and exciting beetroot recipes on the menu.

Beetroot & Cumin Dip with Pitta Crisps

<u>Serves 8</u> • Wheat, gluten and can be dairy-free ⓐ

Heat the olive oil in a small pan and add the chilli, garlic, ground cumin and cumin seeds and fry for 1 minute over medium high heat to soften the flavours. Chop the hot beetroot/beets up and put it into the food processor with the oil mixture and process until smooth. Season the dip with salt and pepper, lime juice and horseradish sauce and mix again. Whizz in the yogurt, adjust the seasoning if necessary and transfer the dip to a serving bowl. Serve warm.

You can chill the dip for a few days but reheat it gently before serving as the fats in the dip become solid and change its texture.

Slice the pitta breads in half and then into triangles. Place them on a non-stick baking tray. Gently brush all over the triangles with the oil, chilli and garlic mix. Bake in the oven until golden and crisp which is about 8 minutes in a hot oven. Drain for a few seconds on paper towels and then serve immediately with the dip.

I love food that is presented individually so I am thrilled to serve the crab in a set of miniature Kilner (glass) jars but if you can only find a bigger one that is fine too, everyone can dip in and share. If you are making the recipe spontaneously on holiday by the seaside then use ramekins of any porcelain or glass dishes. This is the freshest way that I know of to serve our marvellous British fresh crab. You can make it the day before you serve it and it is gorgeous as a starter or equally as a main course for two with salads and gluten-free soda bread or toast.

Potted Crab
in Kilner Jars

Serves 4 or 8
Wheat, gluten and
can be dairy-free

½–1 teaspoon of each; dried fennel seeds, small dried chilli, ground mace, ground nutmeg, depending on taste

2 large fresh dressed crabs (or defrosted if you have previously frozen them)

Zest and juice of 2 unwaxed lemons

255g/9oz lactose-free/goat's butter or dairy-free sunflower spread

Fine sea salt and freshly ground black pepper

Grind the fennel seeds and chilli in a pestle and mortar. Place the prepared crab in a large bowl and mix in all the spices, lemon zest and half the butter or spread. Add the lemon juice to taste and season according to taste. Spoon the crab mixture into clean and dry Kilner (glass) jars or ramekins and smooth over the surface.

Melt the remaining butter or spread, spoon over the top of the crab, seal with the lid (or with cling film/plastic food wrap for the ramekins) and place in the fridge to set. Serve within 36 hours.

This is a really cheap and easy version of a terrine and has been a traditional dish for many centuries in England. The rather cheeky sauce spices up the potted pork and makes a delicious contrast to the meat.

Potted Pork *with* *Chilli* Apple Dip

<u>Serves 6</u> • Wheat, gluten and dairy-free

500g/1lb 1oz butcher's best minced pork

85g/3oz smoked streaky rindless bacon, finely chopped

2 large cloves garlic, crushed

½ teaspoon crumbled mace blades

A sprinkling of freshly grated nutmeg

1 tablespoon chopped fresh thyme leaves

Fine sea salt and freshly ground black pepper

8 juniper berries

4 tablespoons brandy

Bay leaves and juniper berries for decoration

Chilli Apple Dip

1x 450g/1lb jar apple sauce or home-made

1 fresh red mild chilli, deseeded and finely chopped

3 or 4 heaped tablespoons finely chopped fresh coriander/ cilantro leaves

Large pinch of ground cinnamon

Fine sea salt and freshly ground black pepper

You will need a 570ml/20fl oz pudding basin or soufflé dish.

Preheat the oven to 150ºC/130ºC fan/300ºF/Gas Mark 2.

Combine the meats with the garlic, mace, grated nutmeg, thyme, salt and pepper in a mixing bowl. You will need plenty of salt otherwise the pork will be rather bland. Crush the juniper berries in a pestle and mortar or with the tip of a rolling pin and stir them into the mixture along with the brandy.

Pack the mixture into the pudding basin or dish and press down neatly. Press an arrangement of bay leaves and juniper berries in the centre as decoration. Cover with a double layer of foil and twist it under the lip of the pudding basin to make a kind of lid.

Place the dish on a baking tray and cook in the oven for about 1½ hours. Remove from the oven and place some heavy weights on top to compress the meat. Leave the potted pork until cold and then store in the fridge until needed or overnight.

To make the dip: Mix all the ingredients together in a bowl, stir in one tablespoon of cold water at a time until you have the perfect consistency. This will depend on how runny the apple sauce is and if it is home-made or shop bought. Season the dip to taste. Transfer to a serving bowl, cover and chill until needed.

Serve cut in wedges with gluten-free soda bread and the chilli apple dip.

This is a bistro-style dish that can be made for lunch or as a starter. It is literally a movable feast, so you can make it for about 8 people by using all the bread, chutney and a double quantity of ricotta cheese or it is perfect for 2 people with a jar of pear chutney sitting in the store cupboard for next time and the soda bread will last a day or two as will the ricotta cheese.

Wheat, gluten and
can be dairy-free

Ⓢ

My Ricotta Cheese with *Soda Bread &* Speedy Pear *Chutney*

My Ricotta Cheese
Make the ricotta the day before if you like or on the same day. Recipe page 185. (Alternatively, use one or two logs of goat's/sheep's semi-soft cheese with rind or lactose-free semi-hard cheese or dairy-free soya cream cheese-style spread or dip)

Cheese and Sage White Gluten-Free Soda Bread
Make the Cheese and Sage White Gluten-Free Soda Bread on the day. Recipe page 165 (Alternatively, cut ready-made gluten-free bread into thick oval-shaped slices allowing one per person as a starter or two slices for a main course)

Speedy Pear Chutney
Make the Speedy Pear Chutney any day or the same day. Recipe page 174
You will need 1 x 450g/1lb warm, sterilized jam or Kilner (glass) jar for the chutney.
A large packet of wild rocket and a drizzle of olive oil

Make the chutney and fill one prepared jar with chutney, seal and leave to cool before storing in the fridge until needed. Transfer the remaining chutney to a serving bowl and allow to cool while you finish the recipe.

You can serve this recipe in two ways: Either use the soda bread and ricotta combination in which case you should serve a chunk of bread, blob of ricotta, dollop of chutney on a bed of rocket/ arugula. Drizzle the leaves with some oil.

OR

Place thick slices of the store-purchased bread on a non-stick baking tray and toast each side lightly. Meanwhile, arrange the rocket leaves on each plate and drizzle with olive oil. Place a very thick slice of store-purchased cheese or thick blobs of cream cheese-style spread or dip onto each piece of toast and grill until melted or softened. Set the toasted cheese on top of each salad and serve with a dollop of pear chutney to the side.

This is an ideal way to deal with mangled game or just an excess of pheasants in season. It is the simplest terrine that I have come across and the cheapest! I have kept this in the fridge for a week and used it for lunches with salads, chutney, and bread or baked potatoes. It also freezes well. You can use other game birds if pheasants are unavailable.

<u>Serves 10</u>
Wheat, gluten
and dairy-free
Ⓢ

Coarse Game Terrine with *Speedy* Pear Chutney

2 prepared pheasants, meat taken off the bone and chopped into pieces

200g/7oz diced pork fat (from a good butcher)

200g/7oz diced pork shoulder

5 garlic cloves

3 tablespoons in all of fresh thyme, marjoram and also oregano leaves

2 teaspoons allspice

Plenty of freshly grated nutmeg

Sea salt and freshly ground black pepper

Bay leaves

Speedy Pear Chutney (page 174)

Arrange some bay leaves along the base of a terrine mould or a standard, non-stick loaf tin.

Preheat the oven to 170ºC/150ºC fan/325ºF/Gas Mark 3.

Mix all the ingredients together in a food processor and whiz until it has a coarse consistency. Scrape the mixture into the prepared dish or tin.

Cover the terrine with a sheet of non-stick baking paper and then a double layer of foil. Place the terrine in the middle of a roasting tin with 2.5cm/1 inch of hot water in the bottom and cook in the oven for 1½ hours.

Meanwhile, make the Speedy Pear Chutney recipe on page 174.

Remove the terrine from the oven and allow to cool a little before placing some heavy weights or cans on top. This is essential as this will compress the meat and help it all stick together.

Leave the terrine in a cool place for 24 hours before removing the weights and serving with the chutney.

Sounds old fashioned, but not this one! I serve the cocktails in retro sundae glasses or trifle glasses and they look great. Celeriac is a kind of celery and a root vegetable but unlike other root vegetables it stores only a small amount of starch, about 5–6% starch by weight. Like carrots and beetroot, celeriac can also be used raw in salads. The tough surface needs to be sliced off as it is too rough to peel.

Serves 4
Wheat, gluten and
can be dairy-free

Celeriac & Prawn *Cocktail*

½ medium celeriac, peeled

½ lemon, juiced

1 apple, peeled and quartered

200g/7oz generous sized cooked prawns/shrimps (head, tail and shell removed)

2 teaspoons medium curry powder (check label for allergens)

4 tablespoons double goat's cream/lactose-free cream or soya cream

2 teaspoons Dijon mustard (check label for allergens)

Fine sea salt and freshly ground black pepper

2 tablespoons olive oil

2 heaped tablespoons fresh chives or parsley, snipped

Slice the celeriac very thinly and then cut into tiny matchsticks which is a labour of love but worth it. In a large mixing bowl toss the celeriac with the lemon juice which prevents it turning brown. Remove the core from the apple, finely chop the apple and mix with the celeriac. Toss in the prawns/shrimps.

In a small bowl, stir the curry powder, cream, mustard and seasoning together with the olive oil. Toss the curry mixture into the prawn/shrimp salad and mix thoroughly.

Spoon the salads into the glasses and sprinkle with finely snipped herbs and chill until needed.

Tip: if you can't find mustard without allergens, make your own by mixing mustard powder with water but you will only need a quarter of the amount.

Anchovies are part of a family of small, common salt-water forage fish. They are usually classified as oily fish and there are 144 varieties of them swimming around in temperate waters. Unfortunately for the anchovies they are a hot favourite with not only just about every predatory fish around them but also with marine mammals too. Add this to our human consumption as tapas, on pizzas, as paste, flavourings and sauces, it is amazing that there are any left at all. Luckily there are and so here is a delicious recipe for finger food that is perfect served with a glass of chilled dry sherry, white port or white wine.

Serves 4
Wheat, gluten
and dairy-free

Anchovy & Sage Fritters

12 fresh anchovy fillets in olive oil (if using salted ones in a tin/jar, you must drain and then soak them in goat's/sheep's milk or lactose-free milk, or if this is not possible, soak them in cold water for an hour before starting this recipe. This is to remove the excess salt. Drain the anchovies but be careful not to break them)

Zest and juice of 1 unwaxed lemon

24 large fresh sage leaves

Gluten-free plain white flour for dusting sage leaves

Sunflower or rice bran oil for deep-frying

Batter
40g/scant ⅓ cup pure cornflour/cornstarch

40g/⅓ cup gluten-free self-raising white flour blend and extra for dusting

100g/scant ½ cup soda or sparkling water

1 teaspoon rapeseed oil and a pinch of fine sea salt

Marinate the fresh anchovies for at least an hour in the lemon juice and zest. Moisten the sage leaves with a little water and dust both sides with a little flour. Take two sage leaves and sandwich the anchovy fillet between them and squeeze firmly.

In a bowl whisk together the batter ingredients until smooth and to a coating consistency. Line a large flat plate with a thick layer of paper towels.

Pour the oil into a thick-based pan, heat until very hot and then reduce the heat to medium. Dip the prepared anchovy and sage parcels into the batter. Immediately put the parcels into the oil. The fritters should sizzle the moment they enter the hot oil but should not burn. Deep-fry the fritters in 2 batches, turning them over so that they colour evenly. Transfer the cooked fritters to the paper towels and keep hot while you fry up the next batch and then serve them on a clean plate without delay.

These are light fritters that go equally well with an aperitif or as a starter or a light dinner. You can use or make any sort of dipping sauce that you fancy or buy sweet chilli dipping sauce. You can also swap the ingredients to match the seasons, so you can use grated sweet potato, bean sprouts, fresh beans or peas.

Asian *Prawn* Fritters

Makes lots depending
on size of spoonfuls!
Wheat, gluten and
dairy-free

Batter
80ml/⅓ cup water

125ml/½ cup gluten-free beer
or ginger beer or sparkling
water

1 teaspoon fine sea salt and
some freshly ground black
pepper

135g/1 cup rice flour

25g/¼ cup cornflour/cornstarch

2 free-range eggs, beaten

4 tablespoons finely grated
fresh ginger

Filling
175g/1 cup cooked sweetcorn
kernels
4 spring onions/scallions,
sliced very finely

1–2 tablespoons chopped
coriander/cilantro leaves,
parsley or chives

225g/8oz cooked, chopped
prawns/shrimps (heads, shells
and tails removed)

Enough sunflower or rice
bran oil to shallow-fry

Dipping sauce of your choice
(check label for allergens)

Beat all the batter ingredients together in a large bowl until smooth and add all the prepared vegetables, herbs and prawns/shrimp.

Heat the oil in the pan until hot. Lift out medium-sized spoonfuls (the size of a ping pong ball) of the batter, making sure you have prawns/shrimps in the mix. Shallow-fry the fritters on both sides until light, golden and crispy. Drain and serve hot with a saucer or bowl of dipping sauce.

85g/3oz grated courgette/zucchini

Fine sea salt and freshly ground black pepper

400g/14oz cherry vine tomatoes

Olive oil for drizzling

Chorizo, sliced (check label for allergens) – as much as you fancy!

Sunflower/rice bran oil (enough oil to shallow-fry the fritters)

2 ripe avocados, flesh chopped and mixed with the juice of 1 lemon

¼ red onion, very finely chopped

Sprinkling of dried chilli flakes according to taste

3 tablespoons chopped coriander/cilantro leaves

A handful of rocket/arugula leaves per person

Batter
2 large free-range eggs
90g/½ cup gluten-free self-raising white flour blend

30g/1cup finely grated Pecorino sheep's cheese/goat's cheese or dairy-free Parmezano or other pre-grated Parmesan-style cheese

Sprinkle each of cayenne pepper and smoked paprika

60ml/¼ cup plain lactose-free/goat's/sheep's yogurt or dairy-free soya plain set yogurt

2 tablespoons finely chopped fresh coriander/cilantro leaves

175g/1 cup drained canned sweetcorn kernels (or defrosted from frozen)

We love this for Sunday brunch and sometimes we make it with smoked bacon bits instead of chorizo so that it is not so spicy for the children. We buy locally made dried chorizo and it is wonderfully pungent and aromatic but we also use chorizo sausages. The sausages can be chargrilled for extra flavour and then sliced into diagonal chunks.

Corn Fritters *with* Chorizo & Avocado Mash

Serves 3 • Wheat, gluten and can be dairy-free

Put the grated courgette/zucchini in a bowl with a sprinkling of salt and leave for 30 minutes so that their moisture is released.

Put the tomatoes in a non-stick roasting dish and drizzle with oil. Roast them until soft but not mushy. Keep warm until needed.

Meanwhile, slice as much chorizo as you like and fry it in a big thick-based frying pan in just a drizzle of oil and then keep warm until needed. Mash the avocados in a bowl, season to taste, mix in the onion, chilli flakes, chopped coriander/cilantro.

Squeeze the grated courgettes/zucchini in your hands so that all the liquid runs out and place in a large mixing bowl.

Mix all the batter ingredients together in the big bowl with the grated courgette/zucchini and then ladle 3 portions of the mixture into very hot, but not smoking oil in a thick-based and deep frying pan. Fry the fritters until golden on each side and cooked in the middle, mine take about 4 minutes on each side. Keep the fritters hot while you fry up the remaining 3 fritters. I suggest placing them on paper towels briefly.

To assemble the dish: Arrange the rocket/arugula on each plate. Place 2 fritters on top, a scoop of avocado mash, a neat little pile of roasted tomatoes and sprinkling of chorizo.

I love this dish served with new potatoes, fresh mint and a green salad but it can also be an easy and filling starter. Butternut squash is a winter fruit that is usually roasted, baked or mashed and often known as butternut pumpkin. It is full of fibre, minerals and vitamins A and E as well as a cheerful and sunny fruit for winter warmth and comfort.

<u>Serves 6</u>
Wheat, gluten and
can be dairy-free

Crusted Butternut Squash Wedges *with Herb Yogurt*

1 large butternut squash, about 1.8kg/4lb or pumpkin

Olive oil

Fine sea salt and freshly ground black pepper

55g/½ cup white gluten-free breadcrumbs or ready-made brands

3 teaspoons of chopped fresh or dried thyme, oregano leaves or mixed herbs

30g/1 cup finely grated Pecorino sheep's/goat's hard cheese, or 30g/2oz lactose-free hard cheese, grated or dairy-free Parmezano or other brands of pre-grated cheese

Grated zest of 2 unwaxed lemons

2 cloves garlic, crushed

250ml/1 cup or heaped cup plain set Greek-style lactose-free/goat's/sheep's plain yogurt or dairy-free soya set plain yogurt

Plenty of fresh chives and fresh mint leaves, finely chopped

You will need a well-oiled non-stick baking tray.

Preheat the oven to 200ºC/180ºC fan/400ºF/Gas Mark 6.

Trim the top and bottom off the butternut squash and cut in half lengthways. Remove the seeds using a small knife or spoon. Cut each half into wedges about 2cm/ ¾ inch thick. Arrange the wedges on a non-stick roasting tray. Brush liberally with oil, season with salt and pepper and bake in the oven until just cooked through. If using pumpkin, slice it into the same size wedges and remove the seeds in the same way.

In a mixing bowl, combine the breadcrumbs with the herbs, cheese, lemon zest and half the garlic and season lightly.

Remove the baking tray from the oven and press the mix-ture along each wedge and drizzle with a little oil. Return the tray to the oven and bake until the crumbs are golden and the flesh is tender. This usually takes about 15 min-utes in my oven.

Meanwhile, mix the yogurt in a serving bowl with the re-maining crushed garlic, freshly chopped herbs and season to taste. Serve the hot wedges with the herb yogurt.

<u>Tip</u>: you can use the pumpkin seeds if you toast them, they are great on salads and in muesli.

This is such an easy and fun dish for a starter but I also serve it as part of a collection of dishes for a very chilled and laid-back meal. The vibrant contrast of the Beetroot & Cumin Dip recipe page 16 and the Hot Artichoke Dip recipe page 15 is just the ticket for a fun lunch or supper with some light wines and a double ration of Speedy Seeded Flatbreads recipe page 167.

Chargrilled Aubergines
with Tzatziki & Pomegranate Seeds

Serves 4
Wheat, gluten and
can be dairy-free

2 large aubergines/egg plants,
topped and tailed and sliced
thinly lengthwise

Fine sea salt and freshly
ground black pepper

Olive oil

2 cloves garlic, crushed

Dried chilli flakes

Fresh thyme leaves

2 unwaxed lemons, zest and
juice

Tzatziki
250ml/1 cup natural set Greek-
style lactose-free/goat's/sheep's
milk yogurt or dairy-free soya
plain set yogurt

1 tablespoon each of freshly
chopped basil, mint, parsley
and chives

1 large clove garlic, crushed

1 large ripe pomegranate, seeds
scooped out or a 200g/7oz
container of prepared seeds
from a good supermarket

Optional: Gluten-free pitta or
flatbreads (page 167)

You will need a chargrill pan.

Sprinkle salt all over the aubergine slices and leave them to sweat for 30 minutes and then rinse them under cold running water and leave to drain. Pat dry with paper towels and brush each one with olive oil, a little garlic, a few chilli flakes, black pepper and thyme leaves. Fry the aubergine in batches, adding more oil as necessary. Place them on a warm serving dish and keep them warm. When you have finished swill the pan with the lemon zest and juice and sprinkle the mixture all over the aubergines.

Make the tzatziki by mixing all the ingredients together in a serving bowl and season according to taste. Serve the warm aubergines/egg plants, arranged on a large dish with the cold tzatziki piled on top and sprinkle with pomegranate seeds. Accompany the dish with warm gluten-free pitta or flatbreads.

Tip: when cooking aubergines/egg plants avoid serving any that have not been thoroughly cooked through as they will taste bitter.

500g/1lb 1oz minced goat's meat or best lamb mince

1large free-range egg, beaten

1 tablespoon rose water

A large handful of gluten-free breadcrumbs (1 thick, crustless slice)

Mild red chilli, deseeded and finely chopped

1 small red onion, grated

2 heaped tablespoons parsley, trimmed and chopped

½ teaspoon both ground cumin and cloves

¼ teaspoon both ground coriander and cinnamon

¼ teaspoon both ground ginger and smoked paprika

¼ teaspoon both ground mace and nutmeg

¼ teaspoon crushed cardamom

1level teaspoon lavender flowers

1 large clove garlic, crushed

Fine sea salt and freshly ground black pepper

Tzatziki
See recipe on page 29

Gluten-free Pitta breads (available at good supermarkets) or make the Speedy Seeded Flatbreads recipe on page 167

Goat meat is getting more and more popular and can often be found in stalls at farmers' markets as well as speciality butchers around the country. Mince your own meat if it is not sold already minced. I have been on the look-out for a jar of gluten-free Ras El Hanout which is a classic Moroccan rub for lamb and other meats, poultry and fish. It is a complex mix of ground spices and literally means 'top of the shop'. It can contain 30 spices both floral and spicy. So far I have not found one so this recipe is my simplified version of the spice mixture which uses lavender flowers and rose water instead of petals. I combine this dish with the chargrilled aubergine/ egg plant recipe on page 29 for a filling and inexpensive meal reminiscent of holidays in Morocco and Turkey.

Goat or Lamb Minature Koftas *with Tzatziki*

<u>Serves 4</u> • Wheat, gluten and can be dairy-free ⊚

Soak 12 wooden skewers in cold water for 20 minutes so that they don't burn.

Make the tzatziki. Season to taste and chill until ready to serve.

Mix all the kofta ingredients together in a bowl with your clean hands. Form into 12 balls and squish onto the end of skewers to make fat torpedo shapes. Grill them for about 10 minutes turning them so that they are brown all over and cooked through.

Serve the hot koftas with the chilled Tzatziki and hot gluten-free pitta or flatbreads.

You can cook the pears the day before and then gently warm them before assembling the salad. This is a gorgeous winter salad and my favourite starter in the whole book. Watercress is a fast growing semi-aquatic or aquatic plant that grows in chalk streams and is the oldest known leaf vegetable that is consumed by humans. It has hollow stems and floating leaves and I love seeing it swaying in the stream at home. The peppery and tangy flavour of watercress is a perfect foil for other richer ingredients such as strong cheese, oily fish and game birds. Watercress does not store well so use it on the day of purchase to retain the goodness and digestive properties.

Spiced Pears *with* *Roquefort* Salad

Serves 4
Wheat, gluten and
can be dairy-free

250ml/1 cup red wine

100ml/scant ½ cup red wine vinegar

100g/heaped ½ cup unrefined soft brown sugar

1 teaspoon allspice

3 cloves

6 peppercorns

3 large firm pears, peeled and cored and cut into long wedges

150g/5oz fresh watercress, trimmed

Olive oil

Fine sea salt and freshly ground black pepper

200g/7oz Roquefort, other creamy blue sheep's milk cheese/little cubes of lactose-free semi-hard cheese or soya Feta-style cheese cubes

Put the first 6 ingredients in a very large frying pan and simmer gently for 10 minutes until the sugar has dissolved. Add the pear wedges then simmer for 5 minutes, turn them over once and cook for 5 more minutes. Turn off the heat and leave the pears like this for as long as possible so that they absorb as much colour as possible.

To serve, gently heat the pears in the liquid. Toss the watercress in the olive oil and season. Put a small handful of watercress on each plate and sit the pear wedges on top. Dot the salad with little pieces of the cheese and drizzle with the wine syrup.

Serve immediately.

The mixture

½ small onion, very finely chopped

25g/1oz lactose-free/goat's butter or dairy-free sunflower spread

55g/heaped ⅓ cup My Gluten-Free Plain White Flour Blend (see page 181)

250ml/1 cup lactose-free/goat's/sheep's milk or unsweetened dairy-free milk of your choice

125g/4½oz sliced smoked ham, finely diced (check label for allergens)

100g/3½oz lactose-free/sheep's/goat's hard cheese, coarsely grated or dairy-free soya hard cheese

1 teaspoon Dijon mustard (check label for allergens) or make your own from mustard powder and water but use ¼ teaspoon

2 tablespoons goat's double cream/lactose-free double cream or dairy-free soya cream

Fine sea salt and freshly ground black pepper

The coating

2 large free-range eggs

55g/heaped ⅓ cup My Gluten-Free Plain White Flour Blend (see page 181)

150g/1½ cups or more, fine dried gluten-free breadcrumbs (home-made or ready-made)

Sunflower oil, for deep frying

You will need a baking tray lined with non-stick baking paper.

These croquetas are my daughter's favourite tapas, well actually the only tapas she likes! We found a really cool tapas bar in Auckland when we were there for the Cirque de Soleil show but as the croquetas contained gluten I refrained from trying them. So here is my recipe, but now of course gluten-free. You can open-freeze the croquetas until solid and then store in a sealed container interlined with non-stick paper for up to a month.

Ham & Cheese Croquetas

Makes 24 • Wheat, gluten and can be dairy-free Ⓢ

Gently fry the onions in melted butter or spread until golden and soft but not browned. Stir in the flour and cook for about 30 seconds. Gradually add the milk, stirring constantly and cook over low heat for about 5 minutes or until thick and glossy. Stir in the ham and cheese, mustard and cream, and season to taste. Cook for another minute or until the cheese melts, stirring constantly.

Pour into a bowl and cover with cling film/plastic food wrap to stop a skin forming. Leave to cool, chill for 30 minutes. The mixture must be solid.

Take a heaped teaspoon of the mixture and with wet hands, roll into 24 small oval shapes and put on a tray. Beat the eggs in a shallow bowl, put the flour on a plate and half the breadcrumbs in a bowl.

Roll each of the croquetas lightly in flour, then in beaten egg before coating in breadcrumbs. Place on the prepared baking tray. Top up the breadcrumbs and repeat until you have made them all.

Chill the croquetas for 15 minutes in the deep-freeze or pack and freeze until needed.

Deep-fry about 6 of the cold croquetas at a time, using a slotted spoon. Cook them until golden and crispy. Transfer onto a plate lined with a double layer of paper towels to absorb the excess oil and then serve hot.

Tip: make the mixture the day before and chill in the fridge overnight. You will then have the ultimate in fast food.

There are so many different sorts of pesto available now but I love the freshness of this wild garlic version. I drizzle it over salads, use it in the Chargrilled Polenta (page 36) and Gnocchi (page 34) and I often swirl some into my soups.

It can be made fresh between mid-March and mid-June in the UK, after that time the garlic is way past its best and the leaves are discoloured and floppy. If the garlic is not extremely smelly with plenty of fresh-looking bright green leaves then don't make the pesto. You can find patches of wild garlic (ramsons) in the woods and bank sides or if you have a shady woodland garden you could grow your own patch for harvesting. They have pretty clusters of white flowers which can be used as decoration in soups and salads.

When pasta is served with this pesto it really is fast food at its best, due to the fact that wild garlic has 1,700mg manganese per kilo, 17 times higher than common garlic and manganese is needed for building calcium in the bones.

Serves 4
Wheat, gluten and
can be dairy-free

Fettuccine *with* *Wild* Garlic *Pesto*

Wild Garlic Pesto
Makes 2 x 350g/12oz jam
jars 150g/5oz fresh wild
garlic leaves

85g/3oz Pecorino or other
hard sheep's milk/goat's
milk cheese or lactose-free
semi-hard cheese or dairy-
free Parmezano (or other
Parmesan-style grated hard
cheese)

85g/3oz pine nuts

375ml/1½ cups olive oil plus
extra for topping up jar

Fine sea salt and freshly
grated black pepper to taste

500g/1lb 1oz (2 packs)
gluten-free fresh Fettuccine or
400g/14oz dried gluten-free
pasta of your choice

Wash the wild garlic leaves and leave them to dry or use a salad spinner.

Put half the leaves, cheese and pine nuts together in the food processor and pulse until it is coarsely chopped. Add the remaining leaves with all the olive oil, cheese and pine nuts and pulse again until it has the consistency of pesto. Season the pesto to taste with salt and pepper.

Cook the fresh Fettuccine in a large pan of boiling water over medium heat until al dente, about 2–3 minutes. If using dried pasta, cook until al dente but it will take longer than for fresh pasta. Drain and rinse the pasta in a colander and then transfer to a warm serving bowl. A good tip for gluten-free pasta is to rinse it under very hot kettle-boiled water to free it of any sticky liquid while it is draining in the colander.

Transfer the pasta to a hot serving dish, dot with plenty of the wild garlic pesto, toss and serve immediately.

Divide the remaining pesto into clean, sterilized jars, top with extra oil and seal until needed. Keep in the refrigerator but bring to room temperature for serving.

500g/1lb 1oz ready-made gnocchi or make your own as follows:

Gnocchi
500g/1lb 1oz medium-sized potatoes, skin on

100g/3 ½ oz My Gluten-Free Plain White Flour Blend (see page 181)

Fine sea salt

1 free-range egg

1 egg yolk

Extra virgin olive oil

Topping and Sauce
150–200g/5–7oz broccoli florets, trimmed and cut into similar lengths as the gnocchi

Large handful fresh sage leaves

Olive oil for drizzling and frying

Zest of 1 unwaxed lemon

4 tablespoons lactose-free/ double goat's cream, or soya single cream

55g/2oz hard or semi-soft goat's/sheep's milk cheese/ lactose-free semi-hard cheese, coarsely grated or grated Parmesan-style dairy-free cheese

Fine sea salt and freshly ground black pepper

3 tablespoons pine nuts, toasted lightly under the grill

Optional: Freshly grated Pecorino or other sheep's/goat's hard cheese or lactose-free semi-hard cheese grated or grated Parmesan-style dairy-free cheese

Gnocchi is cheap and easy to make and this is the best recipe that I have found in the past 20 years. The only planning needed is the time to bake the potatoes. Don't try to make this recipe with leftover cold potato, it doesn't work! You can make many other delicious sauces but always serve the gnocchi piping hot. The Wild Garlic Pesto (page 33) is also delicious with gnocchi.

Gnocchi with _Broccoli,_ Sage _& Pine_ Nuts

Serves 3 • Wheat, gluten and can be dairy-free Ⓢ

First bake the potatoes until soft.

While they are still warm, press the flesh through a potato ricer into a mixing bowl. Alternatively, scoop out the potatoes and lightly fluff with a fork. Sift the flour onto the potato with the salt and mix lightly with a fork. Then add the egg and the yolk and very gently knead into a ball. Cut the dough into even lengths and roll into long sausages. Cut the dough into 2.5cm/1inch cylinders and carefully place on a floured tray.

Steam the broccoli until al dente. Keep warm. Bring a large pan of water to the boil and drop in the gnocchi. Cook for 2 minutes or until they float to the surface. Carefully remove the gnocchi, drain and then transfer into a warm and shallow serving dish. Leave for 30 seconds to allow them to steam off.

Quickly fry the sage leaves in a little very hot oil and then transfer them onto paper towels.

Drizzle the gnocchi with a dash of oil, toss in the lemon zest, cream and grated cheese, sage leaves and season to taste. Scatter with broccoli, sprinkle over the pine nuts and if you wish, some extra cheese and serve immediately.

The upside to a global recession is we have a growing appreciation of cheaper cuts of meat. Sales of offal in particular are booming but it is a tricky one for a lot of people, including me! However the allure of the thrifty price tag has boosted the renaissance of chicken livers as they are the most approachable of the offal family. They are rich with iron and very quick and easy to cook. If you do not have wild garlic then serve this dish with regular pesto.

Chargrilled Polenta *with* Chicken Livers, *Mushrooms* & Wild *Garlic* Pesto

Serves 4 as starter or
2 as main course
Wheat, gluten and
can be dairy-free

Olive oil

500g/1lb 1oz packet ready-made polenta, cut into 8 slices (check label for allergens)

225g/8oz chestnut mushrooms, peeled and thinly sliced

1 bunch spring onions/scallions, trimmed and finely chopped

Dried chilli flakes

Fine sea salt and freshly ground black pepper

225g/8oz chicken livers, rinsed in cold water, trimmed of any membrane and chopped into bite-sized pieces

125ml/½ cup medium sherry or Marsala

2-4 servings Wild Garlic Pesto (page 33) or ready-made dairy-free pesto

A few basil leaves to decorate

Drizzle a large chargrill pan with oil and set over medium-high heat. When the oil is hot, fry the polenta slices until the outside is golden and crispy with lightly charred lines across each slice. Turn the slices over and cook on the other side. Transfer the polenta onto a hot plate and keep warm.

Use the pan again, drizzle with a little more oil and fry the mushrooms over the same heat. When the mushrooms are softened add the sliced spring onions/scallions, a light sprinkling of chilli flakes, salt and pepper and shake over the heat until cooked. Transfer the mushroom mixture to a hot plate and keep warm.

Use the same pan and drizzle with a little more oil. Fry the prepared chicken livers for a minute and turn them over and fry for a further minute. Slosh in the sherry or Marsala, season to taste and shake over the heat until just cooked. The livers should still be slightly pink in the middle.

To assemble the dish: Place 2 slices of polenta in the centre of each plate. Top with a pile of mushrooms, spring onions/scallions and juices. Scatter with the chicken livers and juices and then drizzle with blobs of pesto. Loosen the pesto with a bit more oil if necessary until you can drizzle the sauce.

Decorate with a few basil leaves and serve immediately.

We ate this utterly delicious tart in Provence last summer, sitting under a vine-clad pergola with views over the hills and gorge. We now have bees which provide us with amazing Manuka honey here in New Zealand but any local honey is perfect for this recipe. This can be a starter or a light main course and makes an interesting picnic idea with other salads.

Sweet Onion, *Honey* & Fresh *Thyme* Tart

Serves 6
Wheat, gluten and
can be dairy-free

(S)

1 x My Gluten-Free Shortcrust Pastry recipe (page 182)

Filling
1kg/2lb 2oz red onions, peeled, root discarded

150g/5oz lactose-free goat's butter or dairy-free sunflower spread

3 tablespoons fresh thyme leaves

Fine sea salt and freshly ground black pepper

1 large clove garlic, crushed

3 tablespoons runny honey

You will need 23cm/9inch fluted, loose-bottomed metal tart tin.

Preheat the oven to 200ºC/180ºC fan/ 400ºF/Gas Mark 6.

Bake the pastry shell blind as in the recipe on page 182.

While the pastry case is baking, make the filling.

Halve the onions and slice them very finely, wafer thin if possible. Melt the butter or spread in a huge, thick-based frying pan and gently cook the onions until nearly soft and golden but do not brown them. Add the thyme, seasoning, garlic and honey and continue to cook until you have a glossy, gooey texture but do not let it catch or burn.

Transfer the mixture into the cooked pastry case and spread it evenly over the base. Cook in the oven for about 20 minutes until hot and browned on top. Serve warm in slices either on its own for a starter or placed on top of a bed of dressed endive and salad herbs as a main course.

Tip: use about half the quantity of dried thyme to the given quantity of fresh thyme as the flavour is much stronger.

We had these Bluff oysters in New Zealand as a fun and delicious starter for a lunch party. This means you can remain standing and chatting which is so much easier these days and proceed to the table for the main course. Sally served them in vodka shot glasses which was a novelty. Everyone loved them and even those who had never eaten an oyster, enjoyed them this way. Make sure the tomato juice is very cold beforehand and keep the glasses in the fridge if possible if the weather or the rooms are very hot. For adults only: you can make them into a Bloody Mary with vodka.

Wheat, gluten and
dairy-free

Sally's Bluff

2 fresh oysters per person, shucked

Your favourite tomato juice

Gluten-free Worcester sauce

Gluten-free chilli sauce

Fine sea salt and freshly ground black pepper

Celery salt

Celery cut into very thin, long matchsticks for decoration

Keep your prepared oysters chilled until ready to serve.

Mix the tomato juice with the sauces and seasonings to taste and chill until needed.

Slip one oyster into each shot glass and pour the tomato juice over it. Nearly to the top of the glass is perfect.

Decorate with the celery stick and serve immediately. Keep the shots chilled in-between servings rather than risk the oysters getting over-warm.

You may not be surprised to hear that middens testify to the prehistoric importance of oysters as food. In the United Kingdom, the town of Whitstable is noted for oyster farming from beds on the Kentish Flats that have been used since Roman times. The town of Colchester holds an annual Oyster Feast each October, at which 'Colchester Natives' are consumed. In Ireland, it is traditional to eat them live with Guinness and buttered brown soda bread.

In the early 19th century, oysters were cheap and throughout the century oyster beds in New York Harbour became the largest source of oysters worldwide. On any day in the late 19th century, six million oysters could be found on barges tied up along the city's waterfront. Extraordinary, when now they are so very expensive and a great treat for special occasions.

My Oysters *Kilpatrick*

Serves 3
Wheat, gluten and can be dairy-free

12 local oysters, shucked/opened

12 oyster shells, cleaned

3 rashers smoked, rindless back bacon (check label for allergens)

Gluten-free Worcester Sauce

A pinch gluten-free breadcrumbs per oyster

A pinch grated lactose-free/goat's/sheep's hard cheese or dairy-free soya cheese

Preheat the grill.

Place an oyster in each shell. Grill the bacon until just crispy. Finely chop the bacon and sprinkle evenly over the oysters. Add a dash of Worcester sauce to each oyster, sprinkle with a pinch of gluten-free breadcrumbs and divide the cheese evenly between them.

Put under the hot grill and cook until the cheese has just started to bubble, this will mean that the oysters are just warmed through.

Serve immediately.

Fish, *Seafood*, Poultry, *Game & Meat*

These bright and colourful-looking pancakes are made with rice flour, turmeric and coconut milk and are traditional Vietnamese pancakes. The crunchy salad served on top of each pancake is a lovely contrast and the dressing is a sharp and yet sweet contrast to the salad. So there is bags of flavour and texture without much cooking; just my scene for a healthy and light dinner.

Vietnamese Pancakes *with* Prawns & Edamame *Bean Salad*

Serves 4
Wheat, gluten
and dairy-free

Pancakes
200g/1½ cups white rice flour

2 small free-range eggs

½ teaspoon fine sea salt

1½ teaspoons ground turmeric

400ml/1½ cups canned coconut milk

2 teaspoons coconut oil, melted

Sunflower or rice bran oil for frying

Dressing
120ml/scant ½ cup fresh lime juice

4 tablespoons toasted sesame oil

2 tablespoons brown sugar

2 tablespoons rice wine vinegar

2 tablespoons Kikkoman gluten-free soy sauce or Meridiana Natural; Sanchi Organic or Clearspring for wheat-free brands

4 teaspoons grated fresh root ginger

contd. >

Make the batter first by placing the rice flour, eggs, salt and turmeric in a large bowl. Slowly add the coconut milk and melted coconut oil, whisking well with a balloon whisk to avoid any lumps. You want the consistency of single cream so add water if necessary. Leave to rest.

Whisk all the dressing ingredients together in a serving bowl and set aside.

Mix all the prepared salad ingredients together in a dish and season lightly with salt and pepper.

You are making 4 thick pancakes. Grease a 23cm/9inch thick-based frying pan with a drizzle of oil and heat over moderate/high heat. Pour in about 1½–2 soup ladles of the batter and swirl around to coat the bottom of the pan.

Once the underside of the pancake is golden then flip it over with a non-stick wide palette knife and carefully using your hands to guide it and cook the other side. Slide each pancake onto a warm plate, pile the salad on top.

Drizzle with the sauce, sprinkle with both the herbs and serve immediately.

1 fresh, mild red chilli, finely chopped or a good pinch of dried chilli flakes

1 large garlic clove, crushed

½ teaspoon fine sea salt

Salad
2 large carrots, peeled and coarsely grated

4 spring onions, finely sliced

100g/3½oz edamame beans, steamed until tender

100g/3½oz mange touts, cut into long, very thin strips

15g/½oz each fresh mint and coriander leaves, finely chopped

100g/3½oz mung bean sprouts

100g/3½oz cooked, peeled prawns, finely chopped

Fine sea salt and freshly ground black pepper

Gravadlax is a simple way of preparing salmon and it is clean tasting and has a remarkable texture. You can use fresh or frozen salmon from a reliable source but wild salmon is best, especially if it is fresh and in season. Make sure it hasn't been hanging around or you may risk an overriding taste of spoilt fish which would be such a shame as it is an expensive dish. The Norwegians call it Gravlaks and Danish refer to it as Gravad Laks and it literally means 'buried salmon' from when it was traditionally buried in dry sand to cure in Scandinavia. You can also use fresh sea trout to make this recipe.

Make the Gravadlax 2 or 3 nights before needed, if possible. This home-made version will last for other meals and sandwiches too. Spare salmon can be used over about 5 days if kept under cover in the fridge. It is divine with gluten-free bagels, or if appropriate, pumpernickel or rye and cream cheese or with hot baked potatoes and sour cream. But it definitely is not very good with scrambled eggs because of the sweet and sour element.

Cured Salmon: *Gravadlax*

Serves 12–24
Wheat, gluten
and dairy-free

1 whole salmon, preferably wild or organic about 2-3kg/4lb 4oz–6lb 6oz (use slightly less of the cure mixture for a smaller salmon or if you are using half a salmon)

The cure
55g/2oz or 2 small bunches fresh dill, finely chopped

115g/1 cup fine sea salt crystals

225g/1¼ cups unrefined caster/superfine sugar

Lots of freshly ground black pepper

You will need a brick or weights to press the salmon and foil.

In a small bowl, mix the cure ingredients together. Lay out a very large sheet of foil and spread ¼ of the cure mixture over a fillet-sized shape in the middle of the foil. Place one fillet on top of this, skin side down. Sprinkle the top of the fillet with half the cure and cover with the second fillet of salmon, skin side up. Scatter the remaining cure on top so you have a huge sandwich.

Wrap the parcel up tightly, tucking the ends and edges in. Put the package in a tray and weigh it down with a brick or something very heavy. Leave this in the fridge and turn the package over after 24 hours. After 48 hours it is ready to eat but you can leave it and keep turning it for another two days.

Unwrap the salmon and wipe off any excess pickling liquid. Slice the salmon thinly with a very sharp knife. For a starter you will need less salmon and you can serve it with the traditional mustard and dill sauce or as a topping for Blinis. Gravadlax is also delicious as part of a main course such as a salad, pasta or in a quiche.

This recipe can be used as a starter or as a main course with a mixed leaf and herb salad. The joy of the recipe is that although it takes time to prepare the salmon, the pancakes can be made 3 days in advance and frozen or made 1 day in advance and chilled. Gravadlax recipe should be made 3 days in advance; recipe is on page 45. As a starter you will need 55g/2oz per person or 100g/3½ oz per person for a main course. The yogurt dip takes minutes to make and the whole dish is served at room temperature and is quick and easy to assemble.

You can serve unwanted pancakes to hungry mouths with jam or lemon juice and sugar. The salmon lasts for at least 5 days in the refrigerator and the yogurt dip can be kept for 2 days covered in the refrigerator and is also delicious with potatoes or salads so nothing will go to waste.

Buckwheat *Pancakes With* Cured Salmon

Serves 8–16 (one pancake each for a starter or two for a main course)
Wheat, gluten and can be dairy-free
Ⓢ

You will need a 20cm/8inch pancake or non-stick frying pan and non-stick baking paper

Gravadlax (page 45)

Batter
255g/1⅔ cups buckwheat flour

3 large free-range eggs

500ml/2 cups almond and coconut milk or just almond milk or any other dairy-free milk

1 tablespoon melted cold-pressed coconut oil, plus extra for frying

Yogurt Herb Dip for 8
500ml/2 cups plain set Greek-style lactose-free/sheep's/goat's yogurt or dairy-free soya plain set yogurt

Plenty of freshly chopped mint, chives, basil leaves

To make the pancakes: In a large bowl, beat all the ingredients together with 250ml/1 cup of water until smooth. Heat the frying pan over medium-high heat. Add a tiny knob of coconut oil and swirl it around and pour off the excess to re-use. Swirl in the batter until you have a perfect circle. I used just short of 80ml/⅓ cup each time.

Fry until golden on each side. Layer the cooked pancakes on sheets of non-stick baking paper for freezing or just pile up on a warm plate. Make the pancakes as shown above on the day or defrost them if previously frozen.

Make the yogurt herb dip on the day: Combine all the ingredients in a bowl and leave to chill.

Prepare the cucumber on the day: Toss the sliced cucumber into a sieve. Sprinkle with the salt, sugar and vinegar and leave to stand for 30 minutes over a bowl. Gently press the cucumber with kitchen paper to remove excess juice. Keep it covered and chilled until needed.

To assemble the dish: Defrost pancakes if previously frozen or reheat if not freshly made by cooking them briefly on both sides in a little melted butter or spread. Place one pancake on each plate, arrange thinly sliced

Cucumber for 8
1 large cucumber, peeled, deseeded and very finely sliced on an angle

1 teaspoon salt

2 teaspoons unrefined caster/ superfine sugar

2 tablespoons cider or balsamic vinegar

<u>*Decoration*</u>
Chopped fresh dill

Wedges of unwaxed lemons

Gravadlax in the centre and top with some cucumber and a dollop of the yogurt herb dip. Sprinkle with a pinch of freshly chopped dill and serve with a little wedge of lemon.

The British crab is not only absolutely delicious, easy to find fresh in any fishmonger and some supermarkets but it is also rather good for you. Many minerals such as iron, zinc and calcium and plenty of vitamins are found in the crab meat but it is also low in fat and calories. This makes for ideal fast food when in season. Crabbing is a popular pastime in British rock pools and around the coastal coves on the beaches. This is a family activity that is fun for all ages, so I wonder why it stops there and that most people don't want to eat them. The brown crab is the one that we tend to eat but spider crabs are good too. Although they have been lurking around oceans, fresh water and tropical waters since the Jurassic times, we British seem to undervalue them and this pot of culinary gold gets sent over to Europe to be eaten by the ton in restaurants and cafés. I hope that we will have a crab revival here and that we will once again see people eating crab sandwiches in pubs around our shores.

Serves 2
Wheat, gluten and
can be dairy-free

Crab *or Crayfish*
& Lemon Spaghetti

200g/7oz gluten-free spaghetti

1 prepared fresh crab in shell/1 heaped cup prepared mixed crab meat or the meat from 1 medium crayfish

Fine sea salt and freshly ground black pepper

Grated zest and the juice 1 unwaxed large lemon or 2 small ones

½ medium, deseeded red chilli, finely chopped or a sprinkling of chilli flakes

4 small spring onions/scallions, trimmed and finely chopped

A handful fresh coriander/ cilantro leaves, chopped

2 tablespoons olive oil

1 tablespoon finely chopped fresh parsley leaves

Bring a pan of water to the boil and cook the pasta until al dente according to the instructions on the packet.

Meanwhile, scrape the crab meat into a mixing bowl and briefly fold in the seasoning, lemon zest and juice, chilli, spring onions and coriander leaves. If you are using crayfish, break up the meat into bite-size pieces and follow the recipe.

Drain the pasta, return to the pan and toss with the oil, toss in the crab or crayfish mixture and warm through briefly. Serve immediately sprinkled with a little dusting of parsley.

The spiciness of the chorizo gives the rabbit a good kick and the wine makes the meat meltingly tender. Rabbit is ideal for people who are not used to the stronger flavours of other game because it is a white meat, low in fat and mild in flavour. Good quality chorizo sausage does not have gluten in it and should just be pure pork, spices, herbs and seasoning.

Rabbit & Chorizo
Casserole

Serves 8
Wheat, gluten and
can be dairy-free

⑤

4 tablespoons My Gluten-Free Plain White Flour Blend (see page 181)

Fine sea salt and freshly ground black pepper

2 large rabbits, jointed into 8 pieces (if frozen, defrost in plenty of time)

1 tablespoon lactose-free/goat's butter or dairy-free sunflower spread

3 tablespoons olive oil

115g/4oz chopped smoked bacon or pancetta lardons (check label for allergens)

255g/9oz baby onions, peeled

8 large garlic cloves, finely chopped

1 bottle red wine

A large bunch of fresh sage leaves

3 bay leaves

1 x 225g/8oz traditional Spanish chorizo sausage (should be gluten-free)

300ml/1¼ cup cold water

Freshly chopped parsley to serve

Preheat the oven to 180ºC/160ºC fan/350ºF/Gas Mark 4.

Season the flour with salt and pepper and dust the rabbit pieces in it. You can use a large plastic bag or a big dish. Heat the butter or spread in a big casserole with the oil over medium heat. Brown the rabbit pieces until golden all over and then put them to one side on a warm plate.

Cook the bacon and onions in the casserole until they are golden and then add the garlic. It doesn't matter if there are some burnt bits as it will add to the flavour. Pour in the wine and give the casserole a good scrape so that any bits mingle with the wine. Add the rabbit, sage and bay leaves, chorizo and cover with the water.

Cook the casserole for about 2 hours or until the meat is tender and falls off the bones. Let the rabbit stew settle and then serve after about 15 minutes with a sprinkling of fresh parsley.

<u>Note</u>: You can make this the day before and reheat in the oven until piping hot with no need for any standing time.

This is an unbelievably easy recipe and so we have it often for lunch with a big salad and warm soda bread. Local, seasonal and ripe tomatoes are of course the best but if they are not in season then good quality vine-ripened organic tomatoes come pretty close. If you have to use smaller tomatoes then slice off the tops and use 8 tomatoes instead.

Beefsteak Tomatoes Stuffed *with* *Garlic* Prawns

Serves 4
Wheat, gluten and
can be dairy-free

4 large beefsteak tomatoes

Olive oil

2 large cloves garlic, finely chopped

225g/8oz fresh or frozen and defrosted prawns/shrimp cut into small pieces

6 heaped tablespoons white allergy-free breadcrumbs

3 tablespoons chopped fresh parsley

Fine sea salt and freshly ground black pepper

Lactose-free/goat's butter or dairy-free sunflower spread

Preheat the oven to 220°C/200°C fan/425°F/Gas Mark 7.

Cut the tomatoes in half horizontally, scoop the seeds out and discard. Place the tomatoes in an ovenproof dish. In a frying pan heat a little oil and gently fry the garlic and prawns until golden but not browned.

Meanwhile, mix the breadcrumbs in a bowl with the parsley and seasoning and then gently mix in the cooked prawns and juices. Stuff the mixture into the tomatoes, dot with butter or spread and bake in the oven for about 20–25 minutes until hot and softened.

This petit poussin recipe can be changed for a couple of small free-range chickens, guinea fowl or pheasants. This dish is pungent, fruity and rather exotic and goes well with a quinoa salad, rice or baby new potatoes. You can use flaked chilli if you don't have any fresh chillies and make up the volume by adding more olives. I keep fresh chillies in the freezer and slice them frozen with a very sharp heavy knife thus avoiding the familiar sight of shrivelled up chillies lurking at the back of the fridge.

Petits Poussins Maroc

Serves 4
Wheat, gluten and
can be dairy-free

2–4 free-range petits poussins (baby chickens). Decide how hungry you and your guests are, do they need a whole chicken each or would they be delighted with half!

100ml/scant ½ cup olive oil

2 large red onions, finely sliced

4 large cloves garlic, finely chopped

4 mild red, orange or yellow chillies, deseeded and sliced in 4 lengthwise (or use 2 medium ones if you prefer)

200g/7oz green olives, drained weight

100g/3½oz capers or caper berries, in wine vinegar, drained

2 x 400g/14oz cans chopped tomatoes

1 large glass white wine

16 fresh mint leaves

Optional: Freshly torn coriander/cilantro leaves

Preheat oven to 180ºC/160ºC fan/350ºF/Gas Mark 4.

Brown the petits poussins in the oil in a very large casserole over medium heat. Then once they are golden coloured all over add the onions and cook for a few minutes. Add the garlic, chillies, olives and capers and lastly the tomatoes and cook for a few more minutes.

Pour over the wine and cook them for about 45 minutes in the oven. Alternatively, you can reduce the heat to low and cook the casserole on the hob for the same amount of time.

The juices should run clear when the meat is cooked through. Let the birds sit for 10 minutes before serving sprinkled with chopped mint leaves. You can also decorate with a flourish of coriander leaves for extra flavour.

This is brilliant for a cook-ahead lunch or dinner party as the cabbage can be made the day before and then reheated during the pheasant cooking process. Pheasants vary enormously and so it is difficult to predict how many they will feed. A tiny one may only feed two whereas a huge fat one definitely three. I use the most enormous Le Creuset iron casserole and so I can get 3–4 birds in. If the birds are very squashed up in any of the dishes then allow extra cooking time and check the legs are cooked through. There is also another recipe for Spiced Red Cabbage on page 79.

Pheasant *with* Red Cabbage & Water Chestnuts

Serves 8–10
Wheat, gluten and
can be dairy-free

2 tablespoons olive oil

2 onions, halved and finely sliced

3 bay leaves

1 large red cabbage, halved, trimmed and shredded

255g/9oz ready-to-eat stoned prunes

3 large cooking apples, peeled, quartered, core removed, roughly chopped

55g/scant ½ cup unrefined dark brown soft sugar

125ml/½ cup red wine vinegar

Fine sea salt and freshly ground black pepper

4 whole cloves and some freshly grated nutmeg

3 pheasants, oven ready

4 thin rashers local back bacon per bird

2 x 225g/8oz cans water chestnuts, drained

55g/2oz lactose-free/goat's butter or dairy-free sunflower spread

Preheat the oven to 180ºC/160ºC fan/350ºF/Gas Mark 4.

Heat the oil in a very large casserole or thick-based pan over medium to low heat. Sweat the onions with the bay leaves for 10 minutes and then stir in the cabbage and let it cook for about 5 minutes before adding the prunes and apples. Stir in 250ml/1 cup of water, sprinkle with sugar, vinegar, salt, black pepper and spices and simmer with the lid on, stirring from time to time until the liquid has evaporated.

Rinse the prepared pheasants in cold running water and pat dry with paper towels. Wrap the bacon along or across the pheasant breasts and top of the legs to protect the meat and keep it moist.

Gently stir the chestnuts into the cabbage so that they are evenly distributed, place the pheasants on top of the cabbage and dot each bird with the butter or spread. Roast the birds in the oven without the lid for 30 minutes. Take a look at the birds and cabbage and if they look moist and fine then continue cooking for about another 30 minutes. If anything looks a bit dry then bring out the casserole, stir and then return to the oven to finish cooking. Take the casserole out of the oven and let the pheasants stand for 15 minutes. Remove the birds onto a carving board and carve. Meanwhile, reheat the cabbage, dot with more butter and heat until it is glossy and sticky.

Serve the pheasant slices and legs if you are using them, on top of a mound of cabbage and juices.

This gloriously easy dish can be made with chicken and is the quickest dinner party dish that I have ever made. You can serve the chicken version out of the game season with rice or new potatoes. In the shooting season I like to serve baked potatoes for ease and speed. This dish does not freeze but I have never actually had any leftovers. Talking of which, leftover Christmas turkey chopped up is also brilliant with the sauce.

Pheasant Indiana

Serves 4 or double
quantities to serve 8
Wheat, gluten and
can be dairy-free

2 cooked pheasants, skin and fat removed, carved into slices and any good leg meat roughly chopped

250ml/1 cup of lactose-free whipping cream/double goat's cream or whipped dairy-free soya cream

4 tablespoons gluten-free Worcester sauce

4 heaped tablespoons mango chutney

Fine sea salt and freshly ground black pepper

Preheat the oven to 200°C/180°C fan/400°F/Gas Mark 6.

Arrange the cooked pheasant meat in a deep ovenproof serving dish. It must be deep because as the cream melts it will overflow if the dish is too shallow.

In a big mixing bowl whip the cream until firm peaks hold; gently fold in the Worcester sauce, chutney and seasoning. If you are using whipped soya cream then it is best to loosen this first with a spot of soya milk and then proceed.

Spoon the sauce all over the pheasant and bake for about 20 minutes until browned and bubbling. Serve immediately or it will dry out.

I love this quick and easy recipe as it is so unusual and rather exotic. My friends are always impressed and ask for the recipe. I advise against using any strong-flavoured honey as it overpowers the other ingredients.

Serves 4
Wheat, gluten
and dairy-free

Chicken *with* Saffron, *Honey* & Hazelnuts

1 large free-range chicken divided into quarters (2 legs with thighs and 2 breasts with wings)

2 onions, roughly chopped

4 tablespoons olive oil

1 teaspoon ground ginger

1 teaspoon ground cinnamon

Generous pinch of saffron strands

Juice and zest 1 unwaxed lemon

4 tablespoons cold water

Plenty of coarse sea salt and freshly ground black pepper

100g/3½oz un-skinned hazelnuts

75g/¼ cup local honey

3 tablespoons rose water

Preheat the oven to190ºC/170ºC fan/375ºF/Gas Mark 5.

In a large dish, mix the chicken pieces with the onions, oil, spices, lemon juice and zest, water and seasoning. Leave to marinate in a cool place, for at least half an hour.

Sprinkle the hazelnuts on a baking tray and watch them like a hawk as you roast them until they are golden. Roughly chop them and set aside.

Transfer the chicken, skin side up, and all the marinade into a roasting tin. Roast the chicken for about 35 minutes. Meanwhile, mix the honey, rose water and nuts together into a paste in a small bowl. Remove the chicken from the oven and spoon the mixture all over the pieces. Return the chicken to the oven and cook for a further 5–10 minutes until the chicken is cooked through and the nuts are brown but not burning.

Let the chicken rest for 10 minutes and then serve.

Feral pigeons live about 3–5 years in the wild or semi-wild; they fly fast at about 50mph and can outmanoeuvre birds of prey. These Rock doves were domesticated for food, as homing pigeons and also bred for their plumage in centuries past. Pigeons are common throughout Europe, the Americas and Asia. Pigeons are always available because they do not migrate and so they are plentiful and easy to find in the butchers.

Serves 4
Wheat, gluten
and dairy-free

Sauté *of* Pigeon Breasts
with Walnut & Orange *Salad*

Dressing
1 teaspoon fresh thyme leaves

1 tablespoon syrup from a jar of stem ginger

1 large clove garlic, finely chopped

1 teaspoon mild mustard (check label for allergens)

Juice and grated zest 1 unwaxed orange

2 tablespoons white wine vinegar

125ml/½ cup sunflower oil and extra for cooking

Fine sea salt and freshly ground black pepper

Ingredients for salad
4 small handfuls of mixed lettuce and herb leaves, washed

2 whole oranges, peeled and pith removed

4 small handfuls of washed and trimmed watercress

4 plump pigeon breasts, defrosted if frozen

24 walnut halves, halved

Make the dressing first by combining all the ingredients and leave until needed.

Arrange the salad leaves on plates. Cut the oranges into segments, remove any pips and arrange the oranges over the salad. Top with watercress.

Fry the pigeon breasts for 3 minutes on each side in a little oil in a frying pan over medium high heat. They should be brown on the outside but very pink on the inside. Transfer the pigeon to a warm plate and let them rest. Add a dash more oil if necessary and fry the walnuts until golden and then sprinkle them over the salads.

Carve the pigeon breast into neat slices and arrange them around the salad or down the centre, however you prefer. Pour any pigeon juices into the frying pan and return to the heat with all the dressing. Stir the dressing for a minute until warmed through and then drizzle over each salad and serve immediately with warm gluten-free pitta or flat breads.

If you make your own mustard it will be stronger so I suggest using about ¼ of the amount.

Simplicity itself but with such depth of taste it is hard to believe that it is so quick to prepare but it is even better if you can leave it to marinate for a few hours or overnight if you find that easier. Tarragon or Dragon's Wort as it is also known, is a perennial herb that is easy to grow in a pot or in a sunny spot by the back door or on the patio. It hates excessive watering, so it is perfect for scatty gardeners like me! French tarragon is considered the best and should be bought in plants and not seeds.

Serves 4
Wheat, gluten
and dairy-free

Lemon & *Tarragon,* Chicken Thighs

4 large free-range chicken leg quarters

6 tarragon sprigs, leaves only

Zest and juice 1 unwaxed lemon

1 tablespoon cider vinegar

2 large garlic cloves, mashed

Freshly ground black pepper

Pinch of cayenne

4 tablespoons olive oil

Preheat the oven to 180°C/160°C fan/350°F/Gas Mark 4.

To make the cooking time even between the leg and the thigh, the bone must be removed from the thigh. This is very easy. Lay the chicken quarter on a chopping board, skin-side down. Run a small sharp knife along both sides of the thigh bone; once the bone is released, cut through the joint between the drumstick and the thigh and discard the bone.

Chop the tarragon coarsely; combine it in a small mixing bowl with all the other ingredients. Transfer the chicken to a baking dish, fill the cavity of each boned thigh with the tarragon mixture and wrap up with the meat and skin. Place the chicken skin-side up in a baking dish and drizzle over all the remaining marinade.

Leave for at least 30 minutes to marinate in a cool place and then bake in the dish for about 25 minutes or until cooked through and the juices run clear.

Let the chicken rest for 10 minutes and then serve with the juices.

Venison is now so popular that New Zealand exports it to England as well as farming venison for the locals. In the United Kingdom, deer farms abound and there are always venison sausages, steaks and joints in our butchers, farmers' market stalls and in the supermarkets. The perception that venison is the healthy red meat option has helped to promote it over the years and chefs all over the world now create masterpieces for lucky diners.

Venison *with Bitter* Chocolate *& Orange* Zest

Serves 4–6
Wheat, gluten and
can be dairy-free

2 tablespoons olive oil

6 rashers rindless, streaky
bacon

725g/1lb 10oz trimmed
venison cubes

1 large onion, thinly sliced

3 cloves garlic, crushed

2 carrots, peeled and finely
chopped

2 tablespoons My Gluten-Free
Plain White Flour Blend (page
181)

750g/3 cups red wine

1 large bay leaf

1 heaped teaspoon each of
fresh rosemary and thyme
leaves

Fine sea salt and freshly
ground black pepper

A touch of freshly grated
nutmeg

25g/1oz dark chocolate (check
label for allergens)

2 teaspoons lactose-free/goat's
butter or dairy-free sunflower
spread

Preheat the oven to 180ºC/160ºC fan/350ºF/Gas Mark 4.

Heat the oil in a thick-based casserole dish and cook the bacon until golden and then transfer the rashers to a chopping board. Brown the venison in the bacon fat and oil mixture and then remove the meat as soon as it is sealed all over. Cook the onions in the fat with the garlic and carrots until the onions have softened. Stir in the flour and cook for a few seconds. Stir in the wine and then add the meat. Chop up the bacon into bite-size bits and add them to the casserole.

Add the herbs and seasoning and cover the casserole with a lid. Bake in the oven for about 1½ hours. Remove the casserole from the oven about halfway through cooking to give it a good stir and see how it is getting on. When the venison is tender and the sauce thick, you can stir in the chocolate and butter and the sauce should become even richer and glazed.

The casserole can be frozen for another time or kept until the next day. When you reheat it, it is a good idea to add some extra liquid such as a dash more wine and some freshly squeezed orange juice and re-glaze.

This recipe works just as well with hogget or mutton and you can use frozen green beans out of season. You can make this the day before needed and reheat when you add the green beans. I have found huge lamb shanks that served two people each but if they are smaller then you can increase the lamb shanks to 4, but stick to the rest of the recipe. You may need to cook the dish for a longer time for older meat or for less time for spring lamb.

Serves 4
Wheat, gluten and
can be dairy-free
Ⓢ

Lamb Shanks *with* *Green* Beans & Feta

2 tablespoons olive oil

2 lamb shanks, 1kg/2lb 2oz total

2 large carrots, chopped

2 red onions, chopped

5 cloves garlic, finely chopped

8–10g bunch fresh thyme

250ml/1 cup red wine

400g/14oz tin chopped tomatoes

1 tablespoon tomato paste

4 bay leaves

Allspice

200ml/¾ cup fresh lamb stock/ bouillon (beef, chicken or vegetable will do)

Fine sea salt and freshly ground black pepper

225g/8oz fine green beans

150g/5oz feta sheep's milk cheese, crumbled or dairy-free soya feta-style cheese cubed

Heat the oil in a huge casserole or heavy-based saucepan and brown the lamb on all sides. Add the carrots, onions and garlic and cook for about 7 minutes over medium heat. Stir occasionally to prevent sticking or burning. Add the thyme and wine and simmer for a couple of minutes before adding the chopped tomatoes, paste, bay leaves and a good sprinkling of allspice. Stir in the stock/bouillon, season with a little salt and pepper and cover the pan with a lid. Simmer the lamb for about 50 minutes, turning it occasionally. If you are cooking hogget or mutton then you will need to cook for much longer and top up the liquids with more wine and stock/bouillon.

Lift out the lamb and leave to rest on a chopping board. Stir the beans into the sauce and cook for 10 minutes or until the beans are al dente. Carve the lamb unless you are serving a small lamb shank per person. Return the lamb to the sauce and adjust the seasoning to taste. Sprinkle with the cheese and serve immediately.

Optional: Serve with warm gluten-free pitta or flat breads or new potatoes with fresh mint.

You can use this Italian dinner party recipe for cooking any joint of pork and it is delicious even if you don't marinate it. Adjust the cooking times according to the type of pork that you cook and how big the peaches are. Pork belly is such an economical roast with crunchy crackling and as the joint is boneless it slices easily too. It is minced for terrines and added in chunks to Asian noodle soups amongst many other recipes. I also serve stuffed baked apples with this pork which makes it rather more suited for Sunday lunch and makes an interesting change from the more usual apple sauce.

Serves 6
Wheat, gluten
and dairy-free

Ⓢ

Roast Belly Pork *with* Peaches *&* Balsamic *Vinegar*

1.6kg/3lb 9oz belly pork in one piece (make sure the butcher has scored the skin for you)

4 large cloves garlic, sliced

12 whole cloves

Grated zest 2 large unwaxed lemons

Fine sea salt and freshly ground black pepper

18 large sage leaves

300ml/1¼ cup white wine

250ml/1cup water

6 ripe peaches, halved, stone removed

Balsamic vinegar and oil

1 tablespoon pure cornflour/ cornstarch mixed with 2 tablespoons cold water

2–3 tablespoons crab apple, rowan, apple and chilli, redcurrant or quince jelly

Preheat the oven to 180ºC/160ºC fan/350ºF/Gas Mark 5.

Take a large roasting tin and place the pork in it skin side down. Cut small slashes with a sharp pointed knife all over the pork flesh and insert the slices of garlic. Stick the cloves all around the flesh too. Spread the pork with the lemon zest and turn it over and sprinkle the skin with salt and pepper.

Tuck the sage leaves under the pork and pour the wine and water into the tin but not onto the pork. Leave to meat to marinate for 12 hours in the fridge or go straight ahead and roast the meat.

Roast the pork for 1½ hours and check if it needs more water or wine about halfway through cooking time. Take the meat out of the oven and transfer it to another roasting tin and leave it to rest. Keep the pan of juices to make the sauce.

Pop the pork back into the oven and roast for another hour to crisp up the skin. Remove the pork from the oven and let it sit for about 15 minutes on a carving board.

While the meat is resting put the peaches in a baking dish and sprinkle them with balsamic vinegar, salt and pepper.

contd. >

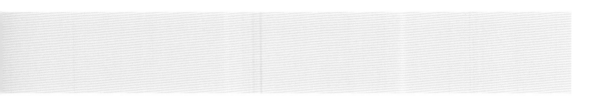

Drizzle with a little oil and roast in the oven until soft but holding their shape.

Meanwhile, combine all the meat juices in one pan, place over moderate heat and bring the liquid to simmering point. Stir in the cornflour/cornstarch and water mix and cook until thick. Adjust the seasoning and stir in the chosen jelly according to taste. Carve the pork and serve with the hot sauce and hot peaches.

This is a wonderful 'Christmassy' dinner party for the winter and I use up all my leftover mincemeat. If you have leftover chestnuts then you can chop them up and add them too, either to the mincemeat or to the sauce.

Mincemeat Stuffed Pork Tenderloins *With* Perry

<u>Serves 8</u>
Wheat, gluten and can be dairy-free

2 large pork tenderloin fillets (about 575-675g/1lb 4oz-1lb 8oz each)

Olive oil for brushing

Lemon juice for brushing

255g/9oz gluten-free sausage meat or good quality butcher's sausages, skinned (I also use Toulouse sausages)

Fine sea salt and freshly ground black pepper

Freshly grated nutmeg and ¼ teaspoon ground cinnamon

Zest of 1 large unwaxed orange

255g/9oz finest quality mincemeat (vegetarian mincemeat is often gluten-free but check the label)

<u>Sauce</u>
250ml/1 cup Perry (pear cider)

2 large bay leaves

2 large cloves garlic, sliced

contd. >

Preheat the oven to 200ºC/180ºC fan/400ºF/Gas Mark 6.

Lay the pork fillet on a large piece of greaseproof paper. You need to open up the tenderloin into a flatter and more even rectangle. To do this slit the tenderloin lengthwise down the middle of the meat, cutting about two thirds of the way through. Cover with another sheet of paper and then carefully bash the meat with a rolling pin from top to bottom to flatten it out a bit. It usually takes me about 4 lots of bashing. Repeat this process with the other tenderloin. Brush the pork with olive oil and then lemon juice.

In a bowl mix the sausage meat with the seasoning, spices, orange zest and mincemeat until combined. Pile the mincemeat mixture on top of one tenderloin and spread evenly. Cover with the remaining tenderloin, secure the ends and then all the way along the meat with string. I suggest tying and knotting the string at 5cm/2inch intervals. Carefully lift the meat into a roasting tin and brush with oil and then lemon juice.

Pour the Perry into the pan but not over the meat. Add a couple of bay leaves and the garlic in the pan and roast for 20 minutes. Carefully pour the stock into the pan of hot juices and cook for another 20 minutes or until the meat is cooked and the juices run clear. Do not over-cook the meat or it will be dry.

250ml/1 cup home-made or instant chicken or vegetable stock/bouillon (check labels for allergens)

1 tablespoon pure cornflour/cornstarch dissolved in 3 tablespoons of Perry

1 heaped tablespoon quince, apple or redcurrant jelly

A large knob of lactose-free/goat's butter or dairy-free sunflower spread

You will need string, greaseproof paper and a rolling pin.

Lift the meat out of the pan and onto a carving board to settle for 10 minutes. Meanwhile, make the sauce by boiling up the juices for a minute or two and scraping around the pan. Remove the bay leaves and garlic. Stir the dissolved cornflour/cornstarch into the sauce until thickened. Turn the heat down to low and stir in the chosen jelly and finally the butter or spread to glaze and thicken. Adjust the seasoning if necessary and then pour the sauce into a warm serving bowl or jug and keep warm.

Carve the meat and serve with the sauce.

It amuses me to think that I lived on a farm in the Goggin, on the Herefordshire borders, surrounded by Hereford cattle in the rolling and lush countryside and now I live in New Zealand on a cattle and sheep farm with Herefordshire beef peering over the hedge at me! So here is my favourite recipe using our delicious beef but any local grass-fed beef that is hung for at least 21 days is going to be fabulous. A couple of good tips are to cut the beef across the grain. You will see small lines running in the same direction, this is the grain. Slice across the grain for maximum tenderness. Secondly, remove the beef from its packaging and bring it to room temperature before cooking as this allows the meat to relax for even cooking.

Serves 2
Wheat, gluten and
can be dairy-free

Beef Tenderloin Fillet with *Quince* Glaze

300g/10oz trimmed beef fillet

2 tablespoons olive oil

Very light sprinkling smoked paprika powder

Fine sea salt and freshly ground black pepper

40g/⅓ cup dried cranberries (I use pomegranate-flavoured sweetened dried cranberries by Ocean Spray, called Craisins)

375ml/1½ cups Gewürztraminer or Riesling white wine

2 heaped tablespoons quince jam/paste/fruit paté or Membrillo

1 heaped tablespoon lactose-free/goat's butter or dairy-free sunflower spread

Preheat the oven to 200ºC/180ºC fan/400ºF/ Gas Mark 6.

Rub the meat with some of the oil and all the paprika and season. Heat a heavy-based frying pan with the remaining oil and sear the meat on all sides. Transfer the meat to a small roasting tin and roast for about 12 minutes for medium-rare. Put the cranberries and 125ml/½ cup of white wine in a small saucepan and simmer for 12 minutes.

Remove the beef from the oven and let it sit while you make the sauce.

Deglaze the frying pan by adding the remaining wine with the simmered wine and cranberry mixture. Shake and simmer the pan for a few minutes. Stir in the quince until the jam has melted. Stir in the butter or spread and then adjust the seasoning. The sauce should be thick and syrupy.

Slice the meat, drizzle with the quince glaze and serve immediately.

This is a cheap and easy dish for lunch or supper and you can treble the ingredients for 6 which will use 225g/8oz of chorizo.

Chorizo is usually from Spain and Portugal and can be a fresh sausage in which case it must be cooked. In Europe it is mainly a fermented cured smoked sausage in which case it can be thinly sliced and eaten without cooking. The fattier versions are better for cooking and the leaner chorizo for tapas.

Serves 2
Wheat, gluten
and dairy-free

Chorizo Hash with *Poached* Eggs

300g/10oz potatoes, peeled weight

Olive oil

85g/3oz good quality chorizo, thinly sliced (should be gluten-free)

1 red chilli, halved, deseeded and finely chopped

Fine sea salt and freshly ground black pepper

A handful of freshly chopped parsley

2 large free-range eggs, poached in water

Boil the potatoes until just tender, drain and cool in a colander so that they dry out a bit. Heat 2 tablespoons of oil in a large frying pan and fry the potatoes until golden and crisp. Add the chorizo, chilli and a sprinkling of salt and pepper. Fry until the chorizo is crisp and then stir through the parsley. Meanwhile, bring a pan of water to simmering point so that you can poach the eggs. While the chorizo is cooking poach the eggs until set. Divide the potato mixture between two warm plates and top each one with a poached egg and serve immediately.

Vegetarian Dishes
& Vegetables

This is such an easy yeast-free dough and makes a delicious pizza in no time at all. You can put any topping on. I had a delicious mixture of fresh fig quarters, gorgonzola, runny honey and rocket on my gluten-free pizza in a restaurant in Wales, which was innovative and fun.

Other ideas such as chorizo and fried mushrooms on wilted spinach leaves or Parma ham, baby roasted tomatoes and roasted sweet red peppers are both delicious. Of course a simple and healthy tomato paste with thinly sliced tomatoes, mozzarella-style cheese and freshly torn basil leaves with a drizzle of olive oil comes up trumps for me too.

Serves 2–3
Wheat, gluten and
can be dairy-free

Quick Flatbread *Pizza*

200g/1½ cups gluten-free self-raising white flour blend, plus extra for rolling

1 heaped teaspoon fresh rosemary, leaves finely chopped

1 teaspoon baking powder (check label for allergens)

A good pinch fine sea salt

200ml/¾ cup plain set lactose-free/sheep's/goat's yogurt or dairy-free soy plain set yogurt

You will need a topping of your choice, olive oil for drizzling and fresh basil leaves are always good on any pizza.

You will need a non-stick baking sheet and 23–25cm/9–10inch base non-stick frying pan.

Make sure you have your toppings ready first. The toppings need to be cooked so that they can just be heated up under the grill or make sure the ingredients are wafer thin and cook very quickly.

To make the pizza: Mix the flour, rosemary, baking powder, salt and yogurt in a big bowl until you have a soft dough. Knead briefly on a floured surface, then cut in half and place each one in a bowl, cover with cling film/plastic food wrap and rest for 20 minutes.

Preheat the grill to high while you roll each pizza dough into two 23–25cm/9–10inch circles.

Oil the frying pan with a good drizzle of oil and heat until hot. Transfer one pizza base to the pan and cook until golden. Flip over the pizza and cook until golden and slightly puffy. Transfer the pizza onto the non-stick sheet and spread with the desired topping. Drizzle with oil, especially around the edges of the pizza. Grill the pizza under the hot grill until your topping is hot and bubbling and the pizza is crispy and brown. Keep the pizza warm in a hot oven until the other one is also cooked and serve them both immediately with an extra drizzle of olive oil.

Not only is the asparagus recipe easy, the flatbreads recipe is speedy and simple too. The mixture of seeds adds a bit of texture and extra taste as well as being nutritious.

Griddled Asparagus & Cheese *with Lemon* Dressing & *Seeded* Flatbreads

<u>Serves 4, with 2 flatbreads each</u>
Wheat, gluten and can be dairy-free

500g/1lb 1oz fresh asparagus, trimmed

100ml/scant ½ cup olive oil

Fine sea salt and freshly ground black pepper

½ unwaxed lemon, zest and juice

1 tablespoon red onion, very finely chopped

A handful chives, chopped

175g/6½ oz your chosen cheese (Halloumi-style that you can slice is best or mozzarella-style cheese, sheep's/goat's/lactose-free or soy cheese)

Speedy Seeded Flatbreads (page 167)

Make the flatbreads first according to the recipe on page 167. Keep them warm.

Cook the asparagus in boiling water until al dente. Drain in a big colander and refresh with cold running water. Leave to drip-dry and that way they will retain their greenness and firmness.

Heat the griddle pan until hot over medium-high heat. Drizzle the asparagus with 2 tablespoons of the oil and sprinkle with salt and pepper and then cook the asparagus until charred all over. This may take about 3–4 minutes. You can do it in two batches if your pan is not big enough. Divide the asparagus between 4 plates. Whisk the remaining oil with the lemon zest and juice, onion, chives and season to taste. Tear, crumble or slice the cheese over the top and drizzle with the dressing. Serve the warm flatbreads with the asparagus.

This recipe is Italian light and healthy fast food at its best. I love it served with a tomato and red onion salad. You can choose to use other vegetables such as sweet roasted red peppers or blanched asparagus tips or a combination of whatever you have left in your fridge.

Courgette & Mozzarella *Piadina*

Serves 2
Wheat, gluten and can be dairy-free

4 small courgettes/zucchini, trimmed

Olive oil

Fine sea salt and freshly ground black pepper

1 teaspoon red wine vinegar

1 small clove garlic, crushed

½ red chilli, deseeded and very finely sliced or tiny pinch of dried chilli flakes

Finely grated zest 1 unwaxed lemon

255g/1¾ cups gluten-free self-raising white flour blend

plus extra for dusting

Mozzarella-style cheese, torn if lactose-free or sliced if dairy-free soy cheese or use sheep's/goat's cheese that you can crumble

Fresh basil leaves

Preheat the grill to high. Slice the courgettes lengthways into thin slices. Drizzle with oil, season and grill for about 5 minutes on each side or until softened and golden. Transfer the vegetables onto a warm dish and sprinkle with the vinegar, garlic, chilli and lemon zest. Season again, drizzle with extra oil and toss.

Meanwhile, make the dough by mixing the flour in a bowl with a generous pinch of salt and some cold water. Add the water a bit at a time until you have a dough-like mixture. Mix with a fork until it starts to come together into a ball and then knead very gently into a soft ball.

Divide into 2 pieces and roll out the dough on a lightly floured surface into two 20cm/8 inch circles. Heat a frying pan over medium heat and then add a good drizzle of oil and one of the dough circles. Brush the top generously with more oil.

Cook on each side or until golden brown in spots and slightly risen. Repeat with the other circle.

Cut each circle in half down the middle with a serrated bread knife. Spoon the cooked courgettes and any juices onto one cut side of each bread circle and top with your chosen cheese and the basil leaves. Top with the other half of the bread and press down gently. Slide one Piadina back into the pan and weigh it down with something heavy like a saucepan or an old fashioned weight and press down gently. Cook for about 3 minutes on each side, replacing the pan or weight each time. This way the Piadina will be golden and the cheese melted. Keep warm while you cook the other one and serve them cut into wedges.

1 tablespoon olive oil

85g/3oz cold lactose-free/goat's butter or dairy-free sunflower spread

1 large red onion, very finely chopped

2 cloves garlic, crushed

Fine sea salt and freshly ground black pepper

225g/8oz Arborio risotto rice

About 1.1litres/2 pints liquid made up of beetroot/beet cooking-water, wine and vegetable stock/bouillon (no more than 285ml/½ pint wine or the flavour will be too strong) – keep the wine separate

4 small-medium cooked and peeled beetroots/beets, cut into small cubes (cook your own with a short stem still on to prevent leaking out of the beautiful ruby red colour) or use ready-prepared but without vinegar

4 heaped tablespoons finely grated hard cheese such as goat's/sheep/lactose-free or dairy-free

2 tablespoons balsamic vinegar

100-150g/3½ oz- 5oz lactose-free cream cheese/soft goat's/sheep's cheese or dairy-free soya cream cheese-style spread or dip

Freshly chopped mint leaves

The gorgeous colour makes a dynamic starter or main course, which can be made the day before and heated up gently with a little extra splash of white wine and knob of butter or spread. As a main course, I serve a green leaf and herb salad and a dish of chargrilled courgettes/zucchini or roasted fennel and asparagus.

Glossy Beetroot *Risotto with* Goat's Cheese *&* Mint

Serves 5 as main or 8 as starter
Wheat, gluten and can be dairy-free

Heat the oil and 25g/1oz butter or spread in a big, heavy-based saucepan and gently cook the onion, garlic, seasoning together until softened. Add the rice to the pan and cook for a minute or two so that it turns translucent and smells slightly nutty. Add the wine that you are going to use and cook until all the liquid has evaporated, stirring frequently to prevent the rice sticking.

Reduce the heat slightly and add a ladleful of the remaining liquids, stir frequently until the liquid has been absorbed. Keep repeating until all the liquid is used up and the rice is cooked but still retains a tiny bit of bite to it. Add the chopped beetroot/beet and balsamic vinegar to the rice when there is only about half a pint of liquid remaining.

Cut the rest of the butter into cubes or use teaspoonful of spread at a time and whisk the fat into the risotto along with the chosen grated cheese. Adjust the seasoning if necessary.

Leave the risotto to rest for a couple of minutes – it should be very glossy by now.

Transfer to a warm serving dish and dot with the chosen cream cheese and chopped mint.

This naturally gluten-free grain is tiny and oval and pronounced 'keen-wah'. Each seed, which can be red or brown, spirals as it cooks because the germ detaches from the kernel. Higher in protein than most other grains it makes great salads but really needs strong flavours and citrus juice or vinegars to liven it up. I serve this salad with Speedy Seeded Flatbreads, so if you want to make the Speedy Seeded Flatbreads first, see page 167 and keep them warm or at room temperature until the salad is ready.

Warm *Quinoa,* *Wild Rice,* Chickpea *&* *Pomegranate Salad*

55g/2oz wild rice, rinsed in a sieve under cold running water

Fine sea salt and freshly ground black pepper

100g/3½oz quinoa, rinsed in a sieve under cold running water

400g/14oz canned or home-cooked chickpeas/garbanzo beans, drained weight

1 ripe pomegranate or 150g/5oz ready-prepared pack of seeds from good supermarkets

½ red onion, finely chopped

1 heaped teaspoon chopped fresh chilli (deseeded) or a good pinch of dried chilli flakes

6 tablespoons chopped fresh coriander/cilantro leaves or finely chopped parsley or a combination of both

Juice of 2 large limes

Dressing

2 teaspoons Dijon mustard (check label for allergens)

2 teaspoons runny honey

1 large clove garlic, crushed

2 tablespoons balsamic vinegar

6 tablespoons olive oil

Serves 6 • Wheat, gluten and dairy-free

Cook the wild rice in a small pan of boiling water until cooked but retaining a bit of bite. Drain in a fine sieve, rinse under fresh water and transfer to the salad dish or bowl.

Meanwhile, make the dressing; whisk all the ingredients together in a measuring jug and when you have a thick emulsion, season to taste with salt and pepper.

Bring the quinoa to boil in a small pan with 500ml/2 cups fresh water and then turn down the heat and simmer until all the grains turn from white to transparent and the spiral-like germ has separated. Drain in a fine sieve, refresh under running water and then transfer to the salad dish or bowl with the rice.

Add the chickpeas, pomegranate seeds, onion, chilli and herbs and mix in gently with the other ingredients. Drizzle the dressing over the salad, pour over the lime juice and adjust the seasoning. Chill and serve with flatbreads (optional).

Please note that if you make up your own mustard from powder, it will be much stronger so you will only need about ¼ of the amount.

This salad is a good crowd pleaser for parties or barbecues and also delicious served as a vegetable accompaniment with hot or cold roast meats or fish. If you are following a gluten-free diet and you are wondering how to get enough fibre then this is a great option as it gives you vegetables, seeds and nuts as well as fibre from the couscous grains.

Couscous Salad *with* Roast Beetroot & Pumpkin

Serves 6–8
Wheat, gluten
and dairy-free
Ⓢ

700g/1½lb pumpkin peeled weight and cut into cubes

700g/1½lb small beetroots/ beets, trimmed weight and cut into similar cubes

4 cloves garlic, crushed

4 tablespoons olive oil

125g/1 cup instant gluten-free couscous, prepared to packet instructions

3 heaped tablespoons pine nuts, lightly toasted

3 tablespoons sesame seeds, lightly toasted

Chopped fresh herbs of your choice (coriander/cilantro, basil, parsley or chives)

Dressing
3 tablespoons olive oil

1 red onion, halved and very finely chopped

1 teaspoon both ground cumin seeds and mixed spice

1 heaped teaspoon soft dark brown sugar

3 tablespoons balsamic vinegar

1 large orange, zest and juice

Preheat the oven to 200ºC/180ºC fan/400ºF/ Gas Mark 6.

Place the prepared pumpkin and beetroot with the garlic and the oil in a roasting tin and toss around so that they are evenly coated. Roast the vegetables until cooked and slightly caramelized. Timings will depend on the size of the cubes.

Make the dressing: Heat the oil in a thick-based, non-stick frying pan and gently cook the onions until softened. Add the remaining ingredients and stir until the sugar dissolves.

Have your couscous ready.

To assemble the salad: Mix the roasted vegetables with the prepared couscous and drizzle with dressing. Top with the toasted pine nuts and sesame seeds and chopped herbs of your choice. Serve warm or cold.

Traditionally red cabbage is made with apples but this version with prunes and apples gives it an extra dimension of flavour and sophistication. I add roast chestnuts or pickled walnuts (check for allergens) to the dish and cook it with roast pheasants for a big party. You can make the cabbage dish a day before you need it, cool the cabbage, cover and chill and it will actually taste even better. I freeze it in two portions but simply halve the amount in the recipe if you are a small party.

Serves 8–12
Wheat, gluten and
can be dairy-free
ⓢ

Spiced Red *Cabbage* *With* Prunes

1 tablespoon olive oil

2 onions, halved and finely sliced

3 bay leaves

1 large red cabbage, halved, trimmed and shredded

255g/9oz ready-to-eat stoned prunes, halved

2 large cooking apples, peeled, quartered, core removed, roughly chopped

55g/scant ½ cup unrefined dark brown sugar

125ml/½ cup red wine vinegar

Fine sea salt and freshly ground black pepper

½ teaspoon ground cloves and freshly grated nutmeg

55g/2oz lactose-free/goat's butter or dairy-free sunflower spread

Heat the oil in a very large casserole or thick-based pan over medium to low heat. Sweat the onions with the bay leaves for 10 minutes and then stir in the cabbage and let it cook for about 5 minutes before adding the prunes and apples. After another 5 minutes stir in 250ml/1cup of water and cover the pan. Leave the cabbage to simmer, stirring occasionally until the liquid has evaporated.

Sprinkle with sugar, vinegar, seasoning and spices and simmer with the lid on, stirring from time to time until the liquid has evaporated.

Dot with the butter or spread and stir until the cabbage is glossy and sticky.

Serve hot or set aside to cool and freeze until needed.

I suggest that if you are reheating the cabbage that you should add some vegetable stock/bouillon and a dash more butter or spread.

This is a perfect dish to accompany roast belly pork or other pork, veal, beef, duck or venison recipes. However, we often have this as a veggie lunch with rocket and other salad leaves and roast tomatoes. You can easily double the size and cook for a bit longer.

Sage & Onion Potato Layer Bake

Serves 4
Wheat, gluten and
can be dairy-free
Ⓢ

2 medium onions, finely sliced

100g/3½oz lactose-free/goat's butter or dairy-free sunflower spread plus extra

1kg/2lb 2oz Desiree potatoes, finely sliced with skin on

Fine sea salt and freshly ground black pepper

8 large sage leaves

115g/4oz grated hard goat's/ sheep's milk cheese or lactose-free/dairy-free soya semi-hard cheese

Cayenne pepper

Grease a 20cm/8inch pie tin or deep spring-form cake tin and line the base with a circle of non-stick paper

Preheat the oven to 200ºC/180ºC fan/400ºF/Gas Mark 6.

Gently cook the onions in the butter or spread in a thick-based frying pan until they are softened but not browned. Arrange the potato slices in an overlapping layer all around the base of the tin starting from the outside and working inwards.

Scatter some onions over the potatoes and season. Lay the sage leaves around the dish and then scatter with some grated cheese. Cover this layer with more potatoes, onions and sage and finish with the remaining cheese.

Sprinkle lightly with cayenne pepper and dot with plenty of butter or spread.

Bake the potatoes in the centre of the oven for about 1½ hours or until the top is crisp and golden and the potatoes soft inside.

Cool in the tin for 10 minutes. If you have used a pie dish then you can turn out the potato cake onto a warm serving plate and then remove the paper before serving. If you have used the spring-release cake tin then you must slide the potato cake off the paper and onto the warm plate to serve.

This winter dish can be made the day before needed and reheated for 25 minutes in a hot oven. It is delicious with any roast game, poultry, sausages or meat. Vegetarians could serve this with a dish of sautéd mushrooms, garlic and parsley. Jerusalem artichokes are not related either to the city or the artichoke but to the sunflower which is rather strange as they don't really taste like artichokes either, more like the sweet, nutty flavour and texture of water chestnuts. They can be used raw in salads and are packed with iron, minerals, vitamin C and they have excellent pro-biotic properties whether raw or cooked.

Serves 6
Wheat, gluten and
can be dairy-free
Ⓢ

Jerusalem Artichoke & Potato *Galette*

85g/3oz lactose-free/goat's butter or dairy-free sunflower spread

700g/1½lb potatoes, peeled weight and very thinly sliced

500-550g/1lb 1oz-1¼lb Jerusalem artichokes, peeled and thinly sliced

Fine sea salt, freshly ground black pepper and freshly grated nutmeg

You will need a 20-23cm/8-9inch deep sided cake tin or Teflon-coated mould.

Preheat the oven to 200ºC/180ºC fan/400ºF/Gas Mark 6. Melt the butter or spread in a pan over low heat and then pour ⅓ of it all over the base of the cake tin.

Neatly arrange the potato slices in tightly packed, overlapping, ever decreasing circles around the base of the cake tin. Follow this with one layer of tightly packed, overlapping artichokes. Season lightly and drizzle with a bit more melted butter or spread. Continue with the final layer of potato slices and drizzle with the remaining butter or spread.

Cook the dish in the centre of the oven for about 50 minutes or until the top is golden brown and the vegetables are soft all the way through.

You can use a skewer to test if they are tender. Let the dish stand for 15 minutes before turning the galette out onto a warm serving plate. You can then cut into wedges to serve with roast meat or other side dish.

This is a stunning mash and everyone has loved it served with local sausages, lamb, pork or veal chops. You can make it in advance so it would be ideal with roast chicken or duck too.

Sweet Potato *&* Ginger *Mash*

Serves 4
Wheat, gluten and
can be dairy-free

1kg/2lb 2oz sweet potatoes,
peeled and chopped into
chunks

About 5cm/2inch knob root
ginger, peeled and finely grated

Plenty of lactose-free/goat's
butter or dairy-free sunflower
spread

Fine sea salt and freshly
ground black pepper

Cook the potatoes in a pan of boiling water until they are soft but not disintegrating. Drain them and return the potatoes to the pan. Mash the potatoes so there are no lumps. Stir in the ginger, butter or spread and seasoning to taste. Serve hot or cool down the mash, cover and chill until needed. Reheat gently, stirring occasionally.

I much prefer this sort of broccoli to the big solid heads of broccoli that you usually find in supermarkets. Long and spindly rather like asparagus and seasonal too. You can make this recipe with both of course and also it is delicious with cooked cauliflower, asparagus or French beans.

Purple Sprouting Broccoli *with* Pecorino *Breadcrumbs*

Serves 4
Wheat, gluten and
can be dairy-free

25g/1oz lactose-free/goat's butter or dairy-free sunflower spread

1 tablespoon olive oil, plus some extra for drizzling

55g/½ cup gluten-free breadcrumbs

Fine sea salt and freshly ground black pepper

1 heaped tablespoon fresh thyme leaves

55g/2oz grated Pecorino or goat's milk hard cheese or lactose-free semi-hard cheese/ dairy-free Parmezano or other brands

400g/14oz purple sprouting broccoli stems, ends trimmed if necessary

Lemon wedges to serve

Heat the butter or spread with the oil in a large frying pan. When the foaming subsides, add the breadcrumbs and stir constantly over medium-high heat until they are crisp and golden looking.

Season the crumbs, stir in the thyme leaves and transfer the crumbs to a bowl. Leave to cool and then sprinkle with the cheese.

Steam the broccoli until al dente, drain and put into a warm serving dish, season lightly and drizzle with a little olive oil. Sprinkle the broccoli with the Pecorino crumbs and serve warm. Garnish with lemon wedges.

Desserts & Puddings

You don't need an ice-cream machine to make the ice creams in this book. At the stage that you would churn the mixture in an ice-cream maker simply freeze in a freezer-safe container. After 2 hours remove from the freezer and beat the ice cream with a fork or balloon whisk until the ice crystals are broken-up and the custard is smooth. Repeat in another 2 hours and then a few hours later beat on the lowest speed with a hand-held electric whisk until the ice cream is silky smooth.

Chilli Chocolate Ice *Cream*

Serves 8
Wheat, gluten and
can be dairy-free

350ml/scant 1½ cups lac-
tose-free whole milk/goat's
or sheep's milk or dairy-free
unsweetened soya milk

1 heaped tablespoon cocoa
powder (check label for
allergens)

6 large eggs, yolks only

125g/¾ cup caster/superfine
sugar

½ –1 red chilli, deseeded and
finely chopped

120–150g/4–5oz dark
continental chocolate 70%
cocoa, broken into pieces
(check label for allergens)

375ml/1½ cups lactose-free/
goat's cream, lightly whipped
or 580ml/20fl oz carton soya
whipped cream

Heat the milk with the cocoa in a saucepan, and then simmer for 5 minutes. Meanwhile using an electric whisk beat the egg yolks and sugar in a bowl until thick and pale and then whisk in the hot milk. Return the pan to a low heat, stirring continuously so that it doesn't curdle. When you have thin custard that coats the back of the wooden spoon you can remove the pan from the heat and add in the chilli and chocolate. Stir occasionally until smooth and thick.

Blitz the chilli chocolate custard in a liquidizer or food processor. Leave to cool but pulse occasionally. Put the cream into a large bowl, ensure that it is only softly whipped and then fold in the chocolate custard.

Transfer the mixture to a freezer container. Put it in the deep freeze following the instructions in the recipe introduction.

Alternatively, transfer the mixture to an ice-cream maker and churn until soft scoop. Serve immediately or freeze in a container until needed.

Commercial ice creams can contain all sorts of additives so there is something very rewarding about making your own ice creams as you know exactly what goes in. You can monitor the sugar for the family and still give them a treat. Ice-cream makers are wonderful as they churn happily on until they produce soft, creamy ices but mine packed up after many years so now I make them all by hand and I enjoy this even more.

This marvellous pudding uses gluten-free stem ginger biscuits or cookies but you could use good old fashioned ginger nut biscuits. You can make the ice cream the week before or even freeze the purée, so it is a gem for weekend entertaining.

Frozen Rhubarb & Ginger Slice

Serves 6–8
Wheat, gluten and
can be dairy-free
ⓢ

500g/1lb 1oz pink rhubarb, cut into chunks

175g/scant 1 cup unrefined caster/superfine sugar

2 tablespoons stem ginger syrup from a jar

200g/7oz or 8–9 gluten-free ginger biscuits, stem ginger cookies or ginger nuts broken-up

375ml/1½ cups lactose-free cream or double goat's cream, lightly whipped or 580ml/20fl oz carton soya whipped cream

Optional: Pink food colouring if rhubarb is rather pale

5 balls of stem ginger, finely chopped

Optional fruit purée to serve with the slices: 225g/8oz frozen summer fruits, semi-thawed or fresh strawberries, hulled

Unrefined caster/superfine sugar and water

You will need a standard loaf tin lined with cling film/plastic food wrap.

Gently cook the rhubarb in a thick-based pan over medium-low heat with the sugar and ginger syrup until just soft. Pour the rhubarb into a large mixing bowl and beat with a wooden spoon or fork until it looks more like a purée. Allow the mixture to cool.

Meanwhile, if you are serving the fruit purée with the slices, then liquidize the berries with a dash of water and sugar and then pass the purée through a sieve to remove any pips. Adjust the sweetness and consistency until perfect, transfer to a jug and chill until needed.

Put the ginger biscuits into a polythene bag and use a rolling pin to crush the biscuits into small pieces but not tiny crumbs or powder. Stir the cold rhubarb into the whipped cream and then fold in the ginger biscuits. If it all looks rather anaemic then you can stir in enough pink or red food colouring to make the mixture pale pink. Fold in the chopped stem ginger. Then pour the mixture into an ice-cream machine until it has the consistency of softly whipped cream. Scrape the mixture into the lined tin and spread evenly. Freeze until solid. Turn out the ice cream and serve cut into slices with a drizzle of fruit purée.

If you do not have an ice-cream machine then simply freeze the mixture in a bowl, beating vigorously every couple of hours with a fork or balloon whisk so that it has a soft and smooth consistency and finally an electric whisk on slow speed and then transfer to the lined tin to freeze solid.

I have made this lovely soft and pretty ice cream with frozen or fresh damsons but you could use blackcurrants just as well. It is a big quantity and lasts for ages in the deep freeze.

Damson & Honey Ice Cream

<u>Makes 2 litres/3½ pints</u>
Wheat, gluten and can be dairy-free

⑤

1kg/2lb 2oz fresh, ripe or frozen damsons, leaves and stalks removed

580ml/2⅓ cups fresh pasteurized whole goat's/sheep's milk, lactose-free whole milk or unsweetened soya milk

85g/⅓ cup mild local honey

8 large free-range egg yolks

175g/ scant cup unrefined caster/superfine sugar

1 tablespoon liquid glucose

500g/2 cups plain set Greek-style lactose-free/goat's/sheep's yogurt or soya plain set yogurt

250ml/1 cup of lactose-free/ double goat's cream, lightly whipped or 300ml/1¼ cup dairy-free soya whipped cream

You will need a sealable 2 litre/3½ pint plastic container with a lid.

Cook the damsons in a heavy-based pan over low heat without liquid, until they are soft. Stir the damsons occasionally to prevent them sticking or burning. Turn off the heat and leave them until cold.

Place the milk in a heavy-based saucepan and bring it just below boiling point over gentle heat. Remove from the heat, stir in the honey and leave it to dissolve and infuse.

Meanwhile, whisk the egg yolks and sugar together in a large bowl until pale and creamy and then whisk in the warm milk. Transfer the mixture into a thick-based saucepan and cook gently, stirring constantly over low heat until the custard starts to thicken. This does take a while but you must not overheat or boil the custard or it will separate. When the custard is thick enough to coat the back of the wooden spoon, remove the pan from the heat and stir constantly for 5 minutes as it continues to cook and thicken. Then stir occasionally until cool and transfer to a large mixing bowl.

Remove the stones from the damsons and discard. Pass the fruit through a sieve or colander and mix the purée into the cold custard. Gently fold in the liquid glucose. Mix the yogurt and cream together in another big bowl. Carefully fold the damson custard into the cream mixture and transfer it into a container to freeze. Beat the ice cream every few hours to eliminate crystals and to ensure a smooth texture. I suggest using a fork or balloon whisk to begin with, and finally an electric whisk on slow speed. It takes a long time to freeze due to the honey and glycerine. Or use an ice-cream machine and when it reaches soft scoop transfer the ice cream to the deep freeze to set firmly.

This recipe works very well with either goat's milk yogurt or sheep's milk yogurt depending on your preference or allergy-needs. Yogurt doesn't freeze on its own so it has to be combined with sugar and other ingredients to freeze in a palatable way. You can use lemon, lime or orange curd instead of passion fruit and it is still heavenly!

Passion Fruit *Curd* *Frozen* Yogurt

Serves 6
Wheat, gluten and
can be lactose-free

320g/11oz Passion Fruit Curd (page 178)

450g/1lb lactose-free/goat's/ sheep's plain set yogurt

250ml/1 cup lactose-free cream/double goat's cream, lightly whipped

55g/½ cup unrefined icing/ confectioner's sugar, sieved

Zest 2 unwaxed lemons

Put all the ingredients together in a bowl in the given order and fold together with a metal spoon. Transfer the mixture to an ice-cream maker and churn until it resembles softly whipped cream. Scoop the ice cream into a sealable container and freeze until needed.

Alternatively if you do not have an ice-cream machine freeze the yogurt mixture in the bowl until it freezes at the edges beating vigorously every couple of hours with a fork or balloon whisk so that it has a soft and smooth consistency and finally an electric whisk on slow speed.

Repeat again and again until you have a consistently smooth and nearly frozen ice cream when you can transfer the mixture to a sealable container.

When plums are in season then this is a sublime pudding. It is delicious served warm with some dairy-free vanilla ice cream or simply by itself. In season you can use peaches, nectarines or apricots.

Plum Queen *of* Puddings

<u>Serves 6</u>
Wheat, gluten and
can be dairy-free

9 large ripe plums, halved and stoned

4 medium free-range eggs

175g/scant 1cup unrefined caster/superfine sugar

Zest 1 unwaxed lemon

15g/½oz lactose-free/goat's softened butter or dairy-free sunflower spread

125g/heaped 1 cup white breadcrumbs made from fresh gluten- or wheat-free bread

500ml/2 cups lactose-free full milk/goat's/sheep's milk or unsweetened dairy-free soya milk

1 teaspoon pure vanilla extract

You will need a well-greased 2 litre/3½ pint oven-proof dish or soufflé dish.

Preheat the oven to 180ºC/160ºC fan/350ºF/Gas Mark 4.

Cut the plums into quarters and place into the prepared dish.

Separate 3 of the eggs (keep the whites to one side) and beat the 3 yolks with 1 whole egg in a large bowl until smooth. Stir in 25g/1oz of the sugar, lemon zest, softened butter or spread, breadcrumbs and milk. Leave to stand for 30 minutes to allow the breadcrumbs to swell. Then spread the mixture gently over the plums.

Bake the pudding on a baking tray in the centre of the oven for about 40 minutes until slightly golden and set. It should still wobble a little bit in the centre.

Whisk the egg whites until stiff and whisk in the remaining sugar bit by bit until you have a thick and glossy meringue. Lastly, beat in the vanilla extract.

Remove the dish from the oven and spoon the meringue carefully over the top into a thick pile. Return the dish to the oven and cook for 20 minutes until the meringue is set and lightly browned.

Surprisingly, this easy pudding will keep for up to 3 days in the fridge and so is an excellent choice for a busy long weekend or holiday. You can make the pudding with eating or cooking apples according to your favourite local varieties and you can cook the apple the day before so that the last minute prep is minimal.

I make this pudding every autumn as soon as I see the windfall apples in the garden because I know that the cobnuts are also ready and can be bought in the farmers' markets or simply picked from the trees in the hedgerows around you. We have enjoyed wild hazelnuts from time immemorial and children played conkers with them. They called the game 'Cobnut' and the winning nut was the cob.

Apple & Cobnut Pudding

<u>Serves 8</u>
Wheat, gluten and can be dairy-free

900g/2lb cooking apples, peeled, cored and sliced (you need to have 750g/1lb 10oz of cooked apple)

55g/scant ⅓ cup soft brown sugar

115g/4oz shelled cobnuts, roughly chopped

115g/4oz lactose-free butter/ goat's butter or dairy-free sunflower spread

115g/¾ cup unrefined caster/ superfine sugar

2 large free-range eggs

115g/1⅓ cup ground almonds

You will need 850ml/1½ pint greased oven-proof baking dish.

Preheat the oven to 180ºC/160ºC fan/350ºF/Gas Mark 4.

Cook the apples gently with 1 tablespoon water and the brown sugar until soft. Or if using sweet eating apples omit the sugar.

Put the cooked apple in the prepared dish and mix in half the chopped cobnuts.

Meanwhile, in a mixing bowl, cream together the butter or spread with the caster sugar until pale and fluffy. Beat in the eggs one by one. Lightly fold in the ground almonds and then spread this mixture evenly over the apples. Sprinkle with the remaining cobnuts and bake the pudding in the centre of the oven for about 55 minutes or until the top is firm to touch and golden.

Serve warm or cold.

Luckily, my friends both in England and New Zealand have quince trees so I have been able to experiment with this wonderfully aromatic fruit. Quince are not usually grown commercially so you won't find many perfect specimens but avoid fruit with soft dark spots. Like pears, quince ripen from the inside out, so later in the season, when you cut them open they may be past their prime. Look for a firm quince, lift it to your nose and if they have a fragrance they should be good for poaching. Over-ripe quince can be made into fragrant jams, jellies and sauces. There is lots of pectin so it's easy to make jars of goodies.

Quince & Pear Crumble

Serves 6
Wheat, gluten and
can be dairy-free
Ⓢ

Fruit filling
1kg/2lb 2oz poached fruit of any combination. I use 500g/1lb 1oz of pears and the same of quince

Crumble
85g/⅔ cup gluten-free plain flour blend

55g/scant ⅓ cup caster/super-fine sugar

30g/⅓ cup ground almonds

55g/2oz lactose-free/goat's softened butter or dairy-free sunflower spread

Finely grated zest 1 unwaxed lemon

2 handfuls pine nuts

You will need an oven-proof deep serving dish.

Preheat the oven to 190ºC/170ºC fan /375ºF/Gas Mark 5.

Peel fruit, remove all stalks, cores and pips then cut into quarters. If the quinces are big then cut them up into the same size as the pear quarters. Bake them with some water or white wine and white sugar or honey or poach the fruit in a pan but either way, cook the quince quarters first as they will take longer. Fill the dish with a well-combined mixture of cooked fruits and level off the top.

Make the crumble: In a mixing bowl, add all the crumble ingredients. Very lightly, with your fingertips, rub the mixture until it resembles breadcrumbs.

Sprinkle the crumble mixture over the fruit and bake in the oven until crisp and golden. I suggest about 25–35 minutes depending on how crunchy you like the crumble but fruit should not be mushy.

We love it served with gluten-free custard or dairy-free vanilla ice cream.

75g/2 ½oz lactose-free/goat's/sheep's butter or dairy-free sunflower spread

115g/¾ cup caster/superfine sugar

900g/2lb can pears, quartered and drained

125g/4½oz dried cranberries or 140g/5oz fresh cranberries

85g/3oz shelled pecans

Cake
115g/4oz lactose-free/goat's butter or dairy-free sunflower spread

200g/1 cup caster/superfine sugar

2 large free-range eggs, separated

2 teaspoons pure vanilla extract

200g/1½ cups white My Gluten-Free Plain White Flour Blend (page 181)

3 teaspoons baking powder (check label for allergens)

185ml/¾ cup lactose-free/goat's/sheep's milk or dairy-free soya milk

You will need a non-stick 30cm/12inch heavy-based, oven-proof sauté pan or Tarte Tatin dish.

Many people think cranberries grow under water since we usually see them floating on the surface. But this is simply wet harvesting where the bog is flooded before the berries are harvested. Growers then use reels, nicknamed 'eggbeaters', to churn the water and loosen the berries from the vine allowing them to float to the surface. There is also dry harvesting using a mechanical picker with metal teeth that combs the vine; this provides the freshest of berries.

Cranberry, *Pecan*, Pear *Upside-Down* Pudding

Serves 10 • Wheat, gluten and can be dairy-free ⓠ

Preheat the oven to 190ºC/170ºC fan/375ºF/Gas Mark 5.

Melt the butter or spread and sugar in the pan over low heat. Meanwhile, pat dry the pears on paper towels. Place the pears on top of the melted butter mixture. Increase the heat and cook until slightly caramelized. Scatter with cranberries and pecans.

For the cake: Cream the butter or spread and sugar and add the egg yolks and vanilla. Mix in half the flour along with the baking powder. Add the milk and then the other half of the flour. Mix gently until smooth. Beat the egg whites until they form peaks and then fold quickly into the cake mix with a large metal spoon.

Gently spread the batter over the fruit and bake in the preheated oven for about 35-40 minutes or until an inserted skewer comes out clean.

Leave the pudding to cool for 10 minutes before turning out onto a serving plate, otherwise the caramelized fruit will stick to the pan. If this does happen, just scrape off the mixture and pack it back onto the top of the pudding. Serve warm.

Peaches came from China and in the East they tend to prefer the low-acid white-fleshed peaches whereas over in the West we prefer the acidic yellow-fleshed peaches. Both are good for this recipe but ensure that they are not at all bruised. This is an excellent way of using up end of season peaches.

If you want to make this dish for 4 people then use two thirds of the jar of maple syrup and freeze the remaining 12 blinis for another time. A good tip is to serve the spare blinis with a softened suitable cream cheese or My Ricotta Cheese (page 185) and a curl of Cured Salmon (page 45) as a tasty starter for four or canapés before dinner.

Serves 8
Wheat, gluten and
can be dairy-free

Griddled Nectarines *with* Blinis & Maple *Syrup*

24 Blinis

55g/scant ½ cup buckwheat flour

55g/scant ½ cup My Gluten-Free Plain White Flour Blend (page 181)

1 teaspoon baking powder (check label for allergens)

1 teaspoon olive oil

2 tablespoons sunflower oil

2 large free-range eggs, beaten

125ml/½ cup water

55g/2oz lactose-free/ goat's butter or dairy-free sunflower spread

Zest 1 unwaxed lemon

4 large, ripe nectarines but not too soft

255g/9oz bottle of maple syrup

A drop of extra oil for cooking

Preheat oven to 180ºC/160ºC fan/350ºF/Gas Mark 4.

Prepare the batter for the blinis: Sift the flours with the baking powder into a bowl, make a well in the centre and pour in the oils and eggs. Stir vigorously with a balloon whisk or fork and gradually incorporate the water. Leave the batter to stand at room temperature for about 15 minutes.

Beat the butter or spread with the lemon zest in a small heatproof bowl and leave to melt for a few minutes in the oven. Halve the nectarines, remove the stones and discard them. Place the fruit cut-side down on a hot griddle or chargrill pan and cook for a few minutes over high heat until they are caramelized on the surface.

Transfer the nectarines, cut-side up into a small baking dish and drizzle with the lemon butter and all of the maple syrup. Roast for about 15 minutes but the fruit must keep its shape.

Meanwhile, make the blinis: Heat a large non-stick frying pan with a drop of extra oil until very hot. Pour a tablespoonful of the blini mixture into the pan and repeat until you have 4 blinis, each about 6cm/2¼inch diameter.

Optional: Serve with a suitable vanilla ice cream

Cook the blinis until they are firm on the underside and bubbling on the upper side, then turn them over and cook the other side. Both sides should be pale gold. Repeat until all the batter is used up, keeping the made blinis warm until needed.

Take 8 warm plates and serve one half of nectarine for each person. Arrange 3 overlapping blinis on each plate, pour the sticky sauce over them and serve immediately with a scoop of vanilla ice cream.

Family fun at its best, children chopping up bananas, smothering them in batter and making toppings or sauces and grown-ups frying the fritters. Nice and messy.

You could also use ripe peach or nectarine slices or mango/pawpaw cubes. We make raspberry or mixed berry sauce by blending the fruit in the liquidizer with some fruit juice. For extreme indulgence we make chocolate or butterscotch sauce. Equally you can simply douse the bananas with maple syrup and sprinkle with ground cinnamon or cocoa powder. Serve with suitable ice cream or sorbet.

Serves 3 or double
quantity for a family
Wheat, gluten
and dairy-free

Easy Banana *Fritters*

40g/scant ⅓ cup pure cornflour/cornstarch

40g/⅓ cup white gluten-free self-raising white flour blend and extra for dusting

100g/½ cup soda or sparkling water

1 teaspoon rapeseed oil

A pinch of fine sea salt

3 ripe medium-sized bananas, peeled and sliced into 2cm/¾ inch chunks at a slight angle

Frying
Extra light/mild olive oil or any other mild tasting oil of your choice

Toppings and Ice cream
Make your chosen sauce or choose your toppings and have them ready. Have your ice cream ready too.

When you are all set and ready to go, whisk together the batter ingredients in a shallow bowl until smooth and to a coating consistency.

Pour sufficient oil to deep fry into a thick-based, deep pan, heat until very hot and then reduce the heat to medium. Dip each chunk of banana into the batter, immediately drop them into the hot oil, they should sizzle the moment they enter the oil but should not burn. Deep-fry the fritters in 2 batches for the smaller amount or 4 batches for the family, turning them over so that they colour evenly. Transfer the banana fritters to a paper towel on a warm plate for a moment or two while you fry up the next batch. Serve them on a clean plate without delay with any toppings or ice cream you have prepared.

This classic and easy pudding could also be made with the many other plums and gages that grow in Europe. The autumn provides a wonderful array of colours with yellow, green or red skinned fruits that are all juicy when ripe. The flesh has equally varying colours and it is fun to change this pudding each time I go to the farmers' market. I have used greengages, yellow gages, and mirabelles in this recipe with great success. As these fruits are generally smaller than large plums you will need a few more than indicated in this recipe.

Individual Plum *Clafoutis*

Serves 6
Wheat, gluten and
can be dairy-free

4 large ripe red plums

3 large free-range eggs, separated

75g/⅓ cup caster/superfine sugar

75g/½ cup My Gluten-Free Plain White Flour Blend (page 181)

2 teaspoons pure vanilla extract

125ml/½ cup lactose-free cream/double goat's cream or soya fresh single cream

A pinch of fine sea salt

Optional: *Icing/confectioner's sugar to dust*

You will need 6 small greased (use a light oil) baking dishes, non-stick tins or large ramekins which must be at least 10cm/4inch diameter and 2cm/¾inch depth.

Line each dish with baking parchment, using a disc shape that comes at least 1.5cm/½inch above the rim of the chosen dish or tin.

Preheat the oven to 170ºC/150ºC fan/ 325ºF/Gas Mark 3.

Halve the plums, remove the stones and cut them into about 6–8 wedges. Arrange half the fruit over the base of the prepared dishes and set aside.

Make the batter: Whisk the egg yolks with half the sugar until thick and pale. You can do this by hand or with an electric mixer. Use a spatula to fold in the flour and then the vanilla extract, cream and salt.

Whisk the egg whites with the remaining sugar until they form stiff peaks and fold them gently into the batter. Pour the batter over the plums until it is about three quarters of the way up the paper sides.

Bake in the oven for 15 minutes and then take the dishes out so that you can arrange the remaining plums on top. Bake for another 5–10 minutes until the filling is set. Remove the dishes from the oven to cool and then carefully remove the clafoutis from the tins and serve each one dusted with a little icing sugar.

Pastry
130g/4½oz lactose-free/goat's/sheep's/butter or dairy-free spread

75g/⅓ cup caster/superfine sugar

1 large free-range egg

65g/½ cup gluten-free self-raising white flour blend

185g/1¼ cups My Gluten-Free Plain White Flour Blend (page 181)

Filling
5 apples, very thinly sliced

Zest 1 large, unwaxed lemon

100g/¾ cup dried fruits mix (sultanas, raisins, currants, citrus peel)

Topping
255g/9oz lactose-free goat's/sheep's cream cheese or My Ricotta Cheese recipe (page 185) or soya dairy-free cream cheese-style dip

45g/¼ cup caster/superfine sugar

1 teaspoon pure vanilla extract

3 large free-range eggs

125ml/½ cup lactose-free/goat's double cream or soya dairy-free cream

1 tablespoon cornflour/cornstarch

You will need a 30cm/12inch loose-bottomed, non-stick metal tart tin.

This apple tart is a delicious change for normal fruit tarts and you could make it using pears instead. Either way, it is easy to make and perfect for a large Sunday lunch, big picnic or barbecue. Different varieties of apples or pears will cook for shorter or longer times and will also vary in overall sweetness.

Baked Apple Cheesecake *Tart*

Serves 12 • Wheat, gluten and can be dairy-free

Preheat the oven to 180ºC/ 160ºC fan/350ºF/Gas Mark 4.

Make the pastry: Cream the butter or spread and sugar together. Add the egg and beat it in and then mix in both the flours. Press the mixture into your tin and chill in the fridge for 15 minutes.

Make the filling by arranging the apple slices in the chilled pastry case. Sprinkle them with lemon zest and dried fruits.

Make the topping by softening the cream cheese in a bowl with the sugar and vanilla. Beat in the eggs, cream and cornflour until the mixture is combined. Pour the mixture over the apples and bake until the apples are just soft and the topping is a light golden brown.

Timings will depend on how thin and ripe the fruit is. It takes about 30–45 minutes in my oven.

A friend of ours has a kiwi fruit orchard on her farm in the South Island of New Zealand and they are so delicious. As they are local and seasonal, we can eat them perfectly ripe which is not always easy in England. The fruit should be firm and plump when you buy them. If they are wrinkled and soft then they are over-ripe and have a strange taste and consistency.

I made this tart in a flash one afternoon with store cupboard ingredients and the only fruit left in the bowl. It turned out to be such a delicious combination that I then made it with the Passion Fruit Curd (page 178) which was sublime but rather expensive.

If you make the tart a day in advance then I suggest glazing the kiwi with a light and clear melted jam/jelly.

Serves 6–8
Wheat, gluten and
can be dairy-free

The Kiwi Experience

1 x My Gluten-Free Shortcrust Pastry (page 182) made in a rectangular, fluted, loose-bottomed, non-stick baking tin/tray 12 x 36cm/4¾ x 14inch. Baked blind, cooled and ready for filling

Filling
255g/9oz sheep's ricotta or lactose-free/goat's soft cheese or dairy-free soya cream cheese-style spread or dip

Enough lactose-free/goat's cream or dairy-free soya cream to loosen the ricotta or cream cheese so that you can fold in the lemon curd

As much ready-made good quality lemon curd as you like (check label for allergens)

4–6 ripe kiwi fruit, peeled and thinly sliced

Place the cooled pastry tart on a suitable serving dish. In a mixing bowl beat the ricotta or cream cheese with a dash of cream until just soft enough to be able to fold in the lemon curd. Fold in the lemon curd with a fork, spread it all over the base of the tart as thickly or thinly as you like. I like it thick to counteract the slight dryness of gluten-free pastry.

Arrange the kiwi fruit in neat lines all over the ricotta/cream cheese mix. Serve at room temperature.

This is a passionate twist on lemon meringue pie for a St Valentine's Day pudding or simply an amazing pudding any time of the year. The purple passion fruit are not exactly local and low air miles for those of us who live anywhere other than the Americas but fruit is in very limited supply in Europe throughout the winter and early spring. The fruit starts off green, ripens to dark purple and the tough rind becomes more and more shrivelled as it ripens into the sweet and sour flavour that we love. The pulp and juices can be frozen until you have enough to make a batch of curd. If you don't want to make your own passion fruit curd you can buy 1-2 jars of passion fruit curd or use a good quality orange curd (check for allergens) with the juice and pips of a couple of passion fruits.

Passion Fruit Curd Meringue Pie

Serves 8–10
Wheat, gluten and can be dairy-free
(S)

Passion fruit curd
12 large ripe passion fruit, halved

4 large free-range eggs

175g/scant 1 cup caster/superfine sugar

115g/4oz lactose-free/goat's butter or dairy-free sunflower spread

1 quantity My Gluten-Free Shortcrust Pastry (page 182)

The meringue
4 large free-range egg whites

200g/1 cup caster/superfine sugar

You will need a 23cm/9inch loose-bottomed metal flan tin, greaseproof paper and baking beans.

Preheat the oven to 200ºC/180ºC fan/400ºF/Gas Mark 6.

First make the passion fruit curd. I used most of it but you can use how much you like depending on how thick you want your filling and if you have managed to resist dipping into it.

Squeeze the fruit into a sieve and push the pulp through to extract about 125ml/½ cup of juice. Reserve the seeds. Set a heatproof bowl over a pan of simmering water.

Combine 3 whole eggs and one egg yolk with the pulp in the bowl and then whisk until warm. Add the sugar and the butter or spread and briefly whisk again.

Use a wooden spoon to stir the mixture over a gentle heat for about 20 minutes or until the mixture coats the back of the spoon. Stir in the seeds. Once the curd looks thick enough to set, remove the bowl from the heat and leave to cool, stirring occasionally.

Make the pastry. Dust the work surface with a little flour and roll out the pastry into a large circle. Line the flan dish with the pastry, trim the edges and chill for 15 minutes.

Line the pastry with a circle of greaseproof paper and baking beans and bake for 20 minutes. Remove the paper

and beans and bake for another 5 minutes until the base is cooked through. Leave to cool slightly while you make the meringue.

Reduce the oven temperature to 180ºC/160ºC fan/350ºF/ Gas Mark 4. Make the meringue. Whisk the egg whites into stiff peaks in a large metal bowl and then gradually whisk in the sugar spoon by spoon until the meringue is stiff, thick and glossy. Fill the pastry shell with as much passion fruit curd as you like and top lightly with swirls of meringue. Work from the pastry edge inwards to the centre. Bake for 20 minutes until the meringue is pale golden in colour. Cool and then chill until needed and serve cold.

<u>Note</u>: Always serve this curd cold or it will be runny!

This is an easy cake to make with most fruits in season such as nectarines, pears, apples, plums and pineapple. It doesn't work with berries or frozen fruit. Caramel is basically burnt sugar but can easily be ruined by multi-tasking as I have recently found out! Some good tips to guarantee caramel success are as follows: do not stir once the syrup has boiled as this encourages crystallization. If the caramel cooks too quickly then plunge the base of the pan into a basin of very cold water and this prevents colouring further. Lastly, if the caramel sets too hard to pour then reheat it over low heat until it melts.

Peach & Caramel Upside-Down *Cake*

Serves 8
Wheat, gluten and
can be dairy-free

Preheat the oven to 180ºC/160ºC fan /350ºF/Gas Mark 4.

Make the caramel first: Place the sugar and water in a heavy-based pan over low heat. Stir constantly to dissolve the sugar; do not allow the liquid to boil until the sugar has dissolved into a clear syrup. Boil the syrup rapidly until golden, swirling the pan frequently so that it colours evenly. Pour immediately into the greased tin.

Arrange the peach quarters, skin side up over the caramel.

To make the cake, sift the flour and baking powder into a large bowl. Add butter or spread, sugar, almonds, eggs and vanilla.

Beat with an electric hand whisk, in a mixing bowl until the mixture is just combined and smooth. Spread the mixture over the fruit and bake until the top is golden brown and firm to the touch. I suggest about 50 minutes.

Leave the cake on a wire rack for about 30 minutes and then run a knife around the sides of the cake and turn out onto a serving dish. If any gooey topping or fruit is left in the tin, simply use a spatula to remove and press it back into place on the cake. Serve warm.

Caramel
175g/scant 1 cup caster/ superfine sugar

6 tablespoons water

2 firm but ripe peaches, cut into quarters (add more if you like)

Cake
155g/1 heaped cup My Gluten-Free Plain White Flour Blend (page 181)

2 teaspoons baking powder (check it is gluten-free)

175g/6oz lactose-free/goat's butter, softened or dairy-free sunflower spread

175g/scant 1cup caster/ superfine sugar

4 tablespoons ground almonds

4 large eggs, beaten

2 teaspoons pure vanilla extract

You will need a 25cm/10inch cake tin, greased.

We grow lots of rhubarb and I find it freezes beautifully. This is a delicious way to use it up and makes a change from normal trifle. If no children are eating it then I add plenty of Cointreau or other orange liqueur.

Rhubarb *Trifle*

1 x Gluten-free Sponge Fingers (page 170)

Rhubarb compote
500g/1lb 1oz pink rhubarb, trimmed weight

75g/⅓ cup caster/superfine sugar

3 balls stem ginger, drained of syrup and finely chopped

1 unwaxed orange, zested and juiced

Trifle
1 sachet powdered gelatine or vegetarian equivalent dissolved in 125ml/½ cup boiled water

500ml/17fl oz carton soya dairy-free custard or home-made cold and thick custard made with lactose-free/goat's/sheep's milk or dairy-free soya or coconut and almond milk

1 teaspoon pure vanilla extract

Medium sweet sherry or Marsala

125ml/½ cup goat's double cream, whipped or 300ml/10fl oz carton of whipping soya cream

A good handful of flaked almonds, toasted lightly

Make the sponge fingers first.

While the sponge fingers are cooling make the compote. Cook the compote ingredients gently over low heat until the rhubarb is just tender but still retaining its shape. Allow to cool.

Meanwhile, prepare the gelatine according to the packet instructions. Put the custard into a big measuring jug or a bowl and stir in the vanilla extract. Whisk in the dissolved gelatine with a small balloon whisk and then leave to chill until the custard thickens up.

Arrange the sponge fingers around the base of a trifle bowl and sprinkle with sherry or Marsala and then gradually build them up the side of the bowl as far as you can, sprinkling with more sherry as you go along.

Spoon over the cold rhubarb compote, work up the sides of the trifle and smooth over. Cover the rhubarb with all the thick, cold custard. Whip the cream until thick and spoon it over the custard. Scatter the almonds over the cream, cover and chill until needed.

What could be more traditional than raspberries and cream? But to ring the changes I have made these tartlets with custard. Not a usual combination I know but with the liqueur added, these little tartlets are divine. The custard is flavoured with Crème de Framboise or you can use Fraises des Bois but cassis is a bit too overpowering so I don't recommend it. If you don't have any of these drinks, then you can use Cointreau. For children omit the alcohol and add pure vanilla paste.

Raspberry *Custard* Tartlets

<u>Makes 12</u>
Wheat, gluten and can be dairy-free

<u>Pastry</u>
1 x My Gluten-Free Shortcrust Pastry (page 182)

<u>Filling</u>
2 heaped tablespoons of gluten-free custard powder mix

1 tablespoon caster/ superfine sugar

60ml/¼ cup goat's/sheep's/ lactose-free milk or dairy-free almond and coconut milk

200ml/¾ cup milk used above

60ml/¼ cup Crème de Framboise

<u>Topping</u>
255g/8oz fresh, hulled, ripe raspberries (never use frozen or canned as they go mushy and leak)

You will need 12 small (6cm/2½inch) loose-base tart tins. Non-stick baking paper and baking ceramic balls.

Make the shortcrust pastry, roll it out and cut to fit the 12 tart tins. Bake blind.

Make the filling by mixing the custard powder, sugar and the 60ml/¼ cup of milk together in a non-stick pan. Stir in the larger amount of milk. Cook gently over low heat until the custard is thick, smooth and glossy. Stir in the Crème de Framboise and beat until smooth again. Cool for 10 minutes and then spoon the custard evenly into the tartlets and smooth over.

Cool for 10 minutes and top with an inspired arrangement of raspberries. Serve at room temperature and eat on the same day.

Delicious served with suitable cream or ice cream too.

Home-made jellies are so easy to make and you can use up any leftover soft berries in the summer and in winter use organic oranges and orange blossom water. Forced rhubarb is lovely and pink by early spring and makes a cheerfully vivid pudding for all age groups. The joy of this recipe is that you only use the juices for this recipe and the pulp can be used for some little individual crumbles in ramekins. Rhubarb has grown all over the world for thousands of years and in China and other countries it was used for medicine and as a laxative but not really for food, as the cost of sugar was so high and it is inedible without. The leaves are toxic and must be thrown away but the long crimson to green stalks can be made into all sorts of savoury and sweet recipes. The crimson or pink speckled stalks are not necessarily sweeter than the more robust and productive green stalks.

Rhubarb & Rose *Jellies*

Makes 4 sundae glasses
or 8 shot glasses
Wheat, gluten
and dairy-free

500g/1lb 1oz pink rhubarb
stalks (trimmed weight),
chopped

100g/½ cup caster/
superfine sugar

1x 14g/½ oz sachet powdered
gelatine or vegetarian
equivalent

1 tablespoon rose water or
more to taste

Poach the rhubarb with the sugar and 500ml/2 cups water until soft and mushy. In a cup, soak the powdered gelatine with 60ml/¼ cup just boiled water. Stir the gelatine until it is dissolved and the liquid is clear.

Carefully strain the hot rhubarb liquid through a large sieve into a big measuring jug.

Stir the dissolved gelatine and then the rose water into the rhubarb liquid and pour it into any glasses you fancy. Leave to set in the fridge and serve chilled. If you are going to keep the jellies for 24 hours then cover them overnight to keep them fresh.

I have heard that there is going to be a world-wide shortage of sustainable chocolate in the next decade due to problems in the Ivory Coast so I am glad that I have been testing all these wonderful chocolate recipes while Fairtrade chocolate is easily available. Any good chocolate from any country is fine for all the recipes in the book but they need to be 70-73% cocoa solids for the best flavour and texture. Stronger and it is overpowering and much less and it will be highly processed and devoid of the true flavours of the different cocoa beans. You can make these squares days ahead and serve with ice cream or with a summer berry compote and cream or poached vanilla pears in winter. You can also freeze them and give them away as gifts.

Chocolate *Truffle* Squares

Makes 60 mini squares
Wheat, gluten and
can be dairy-free

255g/9oz dark chocolate
minimum 70% cocoa solids
(check for allergens)

255g/9oz lactose-free/goat's
butter or dairy-free sunflower
spread, cut into chunks

3 large free-range eggs

A good pinch of fine sea salt

4 tablespoons maple syrup

You will need a 23cm/9inch
non-stick baking tin lined with
baking parchment and a deep
roasting tin.

Preheat the oven to 200ºC/180ºC fan/400ºF/Gas Mark 6.

Break up the chocolate into squares or chunks and melt with the butter or spread in a bowl set over a pan of hot but not boiling water. Over another pan of hot water set a bowl with the eggs and whisk until warm. Turn off the heat and whisk the eggs until thick with a hand-held electric whisk.

Fold the chocolate mixture into the eggs with a metal spoon and stir through the salt and syrup. Pour the mixture into the prepared tin and then place it in the middle of the roasting tin. Pour in enough hot water to come halfway up the side of the cake tin and bake for 20 minutes. Leave to cool at room temperature and then chill for 24 hours before removing from the tin and slicing up into mini squares with a hot knife.

Serve chilled in petit four cases or on a small cake stand.

This is such an easy pudding that I had to include it. It is extremely rich so it is a perfect indulgence for a party. Liquid glucose is a sweet, transparent and viscous syrup which is derived from purified corn starch. It does not crystallize, has a low freezing point and is widely used in the food industry for these reasons.

Italian *Hazelnut &* *Chocolate* Torte

Serves 8
Wheat, gluten and
can be dairy-free

270g/9½oz dark continental chocolate 70% cocoa solids, broken into squares (check for allergens)

250ml/1 cup lactose-free cream/double goat's cream or dairy-free soya cream

1½ tablespoons liquid glucose

3 tablespoons good Cognac

55g/2oz crushed hazelnuts, toasted

4 gluten-free digestive biscuits, broken up

A little melted lactose-free/ goat's butter or dairy-free sunflower spread

Optional: *Cream of your choice to serve; fresh berries in summer or slithers of poached pears in vanilla syrup in winter and decorate either with fresh mint leaves*

You will need a loaf or terrine tin lined with cling film/plastic food wrap.

Set a glass, china or metal bowl over a pan of simmering water over medium to low heat and melt the chocolate, cream, liquid glucose and Cognac together and leave to cool.

Whiz the hazelnuts and biscuits together in a food processor until they resemble fine crumbs. Melt the butter or spread in a small pan and brush the cooled liquid over the cling film so that the crumbs will stick. Sprinkle half the crumb mixture into the prepared tin and tip it around so that the crumbs stick to the sides.

Pour in the chocolate mixture and leave to set for 4 hours or overnight. Just before the torte is set sprinkle with the remaining nut mixture and gently pat down so that they stick.

Leave to chill. Serve just before eating, turn the torte out onto a flat serving dish and cut with a hot knife for perfectly smooth slices.

I love the taste of seriously good chocolate and until recently wondered why it is so expensive. The answer: Apparently it takes a year's crop from one tree which is about 30 pods to make a 500g slab of chocolate. No wonder good chocolate is often sold in 100g bars. This recipe is super easy and fast to make which is why it is a firm favourite in our household. I make it half dark and half milk so that children of all ages enjoy it too but all dark makes an extremely luxurious and dense cake.

This is a brilliant pudding for lunch and dinner parties too as it keeps for days.

A good size cake
for a party
Wheat, gluten and
can be dairy-free

Chocolate *Cake* Extreme

200g/7oz good dark chocolate minimum 70% cocoa solids (check for allergens)

200g/7oz lactose-free/goat's butter or dairy-free sunflower spread

5 medium free-range eggs, beaten

150g/¾ cup caster/superfine sugar

2 tablespoons ground almonds

2 teaspoons pure Madagascan vanilla extract

1 tablespoon My Gluten-Free Plain White Flour Blend (page 181)

Preheat the oven to 180ºC/160ºC fan/350ºF/Gas Mark 4.

Melt the chocolate and butter or spread in a large glass bowl over a pan of simmering water. The mixture will split if it gets too hot so make sure that the bowl does not touch the water. Remove from the heat, stir and leave it for a few minutes.

Stir in the beaten eggs first, a little at a time and then the sugar and almonds, vanilla and flour. Pour the mixture into the prepared cake tin and bake for 20 minutes. Leave to cool in the tin.

Turn the cake out at the very last minute so that it has time to set firm. You can make it a couple of hours before needed or a couple of days, either way it will be luscious.

Totally luscious and naughty but I love the taste of the muscovado sugar instead of normal sugar. I prefer this to other roulade recipes and with no flour at all it is an easy option for allergies. Cocoa powder is much easier and quicker to work with than chocolate in a sponge but I find the taste of real chocolate much better than cocoa powder in the filling.

Chocolate & Muscovado Sugar Swiss Roll

Serves 6–8
Wheat, gluten and can be dairy-free

Sponge
55g/¾ cup cocoa powder (check label for allergens)

Pinch of fine sea salt

3 large free-range eggs

75g/¾ cup dark muscovado sugar

Filling
100g/3½oz chocolate, broken into pieces (check for allergens)

1 tablespoon dark muscovado sugar

1 teaspoon pure vanilla extract

200ml/¾ cup or more lactose-free/goat's double cream, whipped or dairy-free soya whipped cream

Optional decoration and dusting: Icing/confectioner's sugar or cocoa powder

You will need a greased non-stick Swiss roll tin/tray, lined with non-stick baking paper.

Preheat the oven to 200ºC/180ºC fan/400ºF/Gas Mark 6.

Sift the cocoa into a bowl and add the salt. Place the eggs and sugar in a mixing bowl and whisk for about 8 minutes using an electric whisk. The mixture should be pale and mousse-like. Lightly fold in the cocoa powder. Pour the mixture into the prepared tin. Lightly smooth over the mixture with a palette knife. A good tip is to tap the baking tin sharply a couple of times to disperse any large air bubbles in any cake mixture. Bake the sponge for about 8-10 minutes until set and springy to touch.

Lay out a clean tea towel on your work surface and sift over a fine layer of icing/confectioner's sugar or cocoa powder. Turn the cake out onto the surface and carefully roll it up with the tea towel, leaving the paper in place. Do this from the short end so that the Swiss roll will be short and fat. Leave to cool for about 1 hour.

Make the filling by melting the chocolate with the sugar and vanilla and 2 tablespoons of the cream in a heatproof bowl set over a pan of simmering water.

Stir the mixture until smooth and then leave to cool.

Whip the remaining cream and fold the cool chocolate mixture lightly into it.

To assemble: Carefully unroll the sponge and peel off the paper. Spread with the chocolate cream, roll it up again and tip onto a serving plate. Swiss rolls should also be placed seam downwards so that it doesn't unwrap. Decorate as you fancy and chill until needed.

Salt and chocolate work brilliantly together and my favourite chocolates are sea salt caramels so here I have combined the rich smoothness of chocolate with the crunch of praline. The praline is quick and easy to make and you can serve it broken into shards with the Chilli Chocolate Ice Cream (page 86) and the Passion Fruit Curd Frozen Yogurt (page 90). Another idea is to serve the praline shards with either fruit salad or poached fruit. I love to make the praline for gifts at Christmas as the spiciness is festive. But if you cannot make the praline due to allergies then simply serve the mousses on their own.

Chocolate *Olive Oil Mousses*

Serves 6
Wheat, gluten
and dairy-free
◉

200g/7oz dark chocolate minimum 70% cocoa solids (check for allergens)

80ml/⅓ cup light olive oil

5 large free-range eggs, separated

Large pinch of fine sea salt

160g/scant 1 cup caster/superfine sugar

Sesame, Salt and Chilli Praline

200g/1 cup caster/superfine/granulated sugar

30g/1oz sesame seeds

1 teaspoon fine sea salt flakes, or more if you like (2 maximum)

1 mild red chilli, deseeded and very finely chopped or a tiny scattering of dried chilli flakes

You will need 6 large ramekins and a baking tray lined with non-stick baking paper.

Set a heatproof bowl over a pan of simmering water, melt the chocolate and slowly stir in the olive oil. Beat the egg yolks with half the sugar in a big bowl until pale and fluffy. Stir in the chocolate mix. Whisk the egg whites and salt together in a clean bowl until they are stiff. Continue to whisk the eggs as you add the remaining sugar a bit at a time. Fold the egg white mix into the chocolate mix.

Spoon the mixture into the ramekins, smooth over the tops and chill overnight.

The next day make the praline; put the sugar in a thick-based, medium pan over low heat until it is melted and golden brown. Remove from the heat and immediately stir in the seeds, salt and chilli. Quickly pour the mixture evenly over the paper-lined baking tray. When the praline is cold and hard break it up into shards that you can dig into each mousse. I use two shards for each one.

To serve, place a mousse on a small plate with a few extra shards on the side.

This is such a simple cake to make and you can ice it any way you want to for any occasion. Fill it with stiffly whipped cream with Dulce de Leche blobs folded in or fill with ice cream of your choice and layers of Dulce de Leche as in the recipe below. If you cannot find a can of the ready-made dairy-free Dulce de Leche, you can create your own version by making the Confiture de Lait (page 175). I have not given the quantities for the chocolate sauce as I don't know how many people you will be serving.

Celebration *Chocolate* & *Ice Cream* Cake

<u>A good size cake for a party</u>
Wheat, gluten and can be dairy-free

340g/12oz can Soymilke Dulce de Leche flavour

1 or 2 tubs dairy-free vanilla ice cream (depending on how big you want the cake to be). I use two

<u>Cake</u>
175g/6oz lactose-free goat's butter or dairy-free sunflower spread

175g/1½ cups soft brown sugar

3 large free-range eggs

175g/1¼ cups plain gluten-free flour blend, sifted

115g/4oz melted dark chocolate (check for allergens)

1 tablespoon coffee essence or dissolved coffee powder

2 teaspoons baking powder (check label for allergens)

<u>Chocolate sauce</u>
Whatever chocolate you like (check for allergens), broken into pieces or squares or use buttons

Preheat oven to 190ºC/170ºC fan/375ºF/Gas Mark 5.

To make the cake, beat the butter or spread with the sugar in a large mixing bowl until light and soft. Add one egg at a time, lightly beating it in. Fold in a bit of the flour and repeat until all the eggs and the flour is used up. Stir in the melted chocolate and liquid coffee. Fold in the baking powder and then transfer the mixture to the prepared tins.

Dip the centre slightly so that the top of each cake is flat when it is cooked as this will make it easier to fill with ice cream.

Bake the cake for about 20 minutes or until just springy to the touch. Cool the cake and then turn out on to a wire rack to cool completely. Lightly ice the top of the cake with chocolate icing if you wish or leave it as it is and dust with sifted cocoa powder just before serving.

Meanwhile, make as much chocolate sauce as you need by placing your chocolate pieces with a knob of butter or spread, a dash of hot, black coffee and a dash of brandy if you fancy in a heatproof bowl over a pan of simmering water. Stir until melted, thick and glossy. Keep warm until needed.

At the last minute, assemble the cake by placing the bottom sponge on a cake stand or serving plate. Spread this sponge with half the Dulce de Leche. Pile on the ice

A knob of lactose-free/goat's butter or dairy-free sunflower spread

A little hot black coffee

A dash of good brandy if you fancy (not for children)

<u>Optional</u>: Chocolate icing for the top of the cake or sifted cocoa powder

You will need 2 x 23cm/9inch non-stick round cake tins, greased and lined.

cream and level it off. Top with blobs of the remaining Dulce de Leche. Cover with the second sponge and dust with sifted cocoa powder. Serve immediately with the warm chocolate sauce.

These little wisps of perfection have become widely available recently but just a few years ago you could only buy macarons at a French pâtisserie. We now see them on stalls at local farmers' markets as well as in fancy shopping malls at coffee stands and there are entire books dedicated to the art of making them. You can change the flavour of these macarons by adding 2 tablespoons of very strong dissolved and cooled instant coffee or espresso coffee instead of water. Please note that you can store the macarons for a few days or a weekend in an air-tight container as long as they are unfilled.

Macarons *with* *Confiture* De Lait

Makes 36
Wheat, gluten and can be dairy-free

Macarons
125g/1 cup icing/confectioner's sugar

125g/scant 1⅓ cups ground almonds

90g/3oz free-range egg whites

2 tablespoons water

110g/heaped ½ cup caster/superfine sugar

Filling
Make Confiture de Lait (page 172) up to 2 weeks in advance or buy a 340g/12oz can of Soymilke Dulce de Leche flavour

Lactose-free/goat's/sheep's cream cheese mixed with enough lactose-free/goat's/sheep's milk to make a soft peak filling.

or dairy-free soya cream cheese-style dip mixed with enough dairy-free milk to make a soft peak filling. The amount needed will depend

Preheat the oven to 170ºC/150ºC fan/325ºF/Gas Mark 3.

Put the icing sugar, ground almonds and 40g/1½oz egg whites together in a large bowl and mix to a paste.

Put the water and caster sugar in a small pan and heat gently to melt the sugar. When dissolved, turn up the heat and boil until the syrup thickens.

Whisk the remaining 50g/2oz egg whites in a bowl until medium-stiff peaks form when you lift out the whisk. Pour in the syrup, whisking all the time until stiff and shiny. If you are colouring or flavouring the macarons, now is the time. Gently combine the meringue mixture with the almond paste mixture and stir until it is stiff and shiny again.

Spoon the mixture into a piping bag and pipe small flat circles approx 4cm/1½inch onto the macaron mats, on the baking sheets or onto baking paper on baking sheets. To make things easier you can draw circles onto the baking paper and pipe into the centre of each circle. The piping will leave a small 'tip' on each circle, so you will need to give the trays a shake at the end to flatten them.

Leave to stand for 30 minutes to form a skin and then bake them for about 12 minutes until firm and pale. Remove the trays from the oven and leave to cool slightly

on the type of cream cheese you are using.

You will need macaron rubber mats and piping set or baking sheets, lined with baking paper and a regular piping bag.

before transferring the mats to a cool surface. When the macarons are cold you can peel them off. If you are using baking paper, keep the macarons on the paper until cold and then lift them off to fill them.

Spread one macaron very lightly with the cream cheese mixture and some confiture de lait and sandwich with another macaron. Serve them or keep for a day in a cool place.

I am so anti the endless boxes of breakfast cereal that fill children and adults alike with too much sugar and salt. Nothing delights children more than a pile of hot pancakes with a thick drizzle of honey or maple syrup. They take minutes to make and everyone sits round the table in a buzz of expectation and the reward for a brief effort is a table-full of happy faces. A pile of ripe berries and yogurt alongside makes it a nutritious as well as filling breakfast but this recipe is also delicious as a pudding any day of the week for children and adults alike.

Interestingly buckwheat is not technically a grain; it has gained entry into the wholegrain group because of its appearance and robust flavour. It is in fact a relation of the rhubarb and a member of the grass family. The seeds, known as groats, are triangular in shape and can be toasted before cooking and they are then known as kasha. Buckwheat flour is used for blinis and soba noodles as well as these delicious pancakes.

Makes 8–10
Wheat, gluten and
can be dairy-free

Buckwheat *Pancakes* *with* Confiture *De Lait*

275ml/9½fl oz lactose-free/goat's/sheep's milk or dairy-free soya milk

1 large free-range egg

Pinch of fine sea salt

1 teaspoon vegetable oil

110g/¾ cup buckwheat flour

Vegetable oil, for cooking

• You can serve with Confiture de Lait (page 172) made up to 2 weeks in advance, honey or maple syrup or serve with suitable vanilla ice cream as a pudding.

Place the milk, egg, salt and oil into a large bowl and mix well.

Sift the buckwheat flour into a separate bowl.

Whisk the flour into the milk mixture gradually, stirring constantly until a smooth batter is formed. Allow the batter to rest for 30 minutes prior to cooking.

Brush a non-stick frying or pancake pan with a little oil, heat over medium-high heat and then pour in an eighth of the mixture. Swirl the pancake mix around until you have a perfect thin round pancake. Cook for a few minutes on both sides or until golden on each side. Spread lightly with confiture de lait, if using or a filling of your choice. Flip over half the pancake and then flip again onto the other side. After a few moments, when the filling is warmed through, remove the pancake from the pan and serve hot with berries and yogurt for breakfast or with a scoop of suitable vanilla ice cream for pudding.

Tip: make the pancakes but cook them lightly. Place each one between sheets of non-stick baking paper. Repeat the process with the remaining mixture to create eight to ten pancakes. You can freeze them at this point, defrost them, reheat them, fill them and serve.

Fabulously naughty but worth every mouthful. Keep it chilled or the caramel will melt. If you don't finish it for pudding then it is great for afternoon tea or with a shot of mid-morning coffee. This is a New Zealand recipe that I have adapted to be gluten and dairy friendly.

Caramel Meringue *Slice*

Makes 16–20 pieces
Wheat, gluten and
can be dairy-free

150g/5oz lactose-free/goat's butter, softened or dairy-free sunflower spread

2 tablespoons caster/ superfine sugar

1 large free-range egg

225g/1½ cups gluten-free plain flour blend

1 heaped teaspoon baking powder (check label for allergens)

Filling
340g/12oz can of Soymilke Dulce de Leche flavour

Or about 400g/12oz Confiture de Lait (page 172)

Meringue
3 large free-range egg whites

6 heaped tablespoons caster/ superfine sugar

You will need a lined 20cm x 30cm/8 x 12inch rectangular, deep-sided, non-stick baking tin.

Preheat the oven to 180°C/160°C fan/350°F/Gas Mark 4.

Make the base first: Cream the butter or spread with the sugar until pale and then beat in the egg. Sift the flour and baking powder together and mix until well combined. Press the mixture into the tin, making sure it is even.

Bake for about 20 minutes or until golden. Remove from the oven and leave to cool. When the base is just warm, spread over the Dulce de Leche.

Make the meringue: Beat the egg whites until stiff and gradually add the sugar, beating with an electric whisk all the time until the meringue is thick and glossy.

Spoon the meringue over the caramel and bake in the oven for about 20 minutes or until the meringue is golden. Leave to cool in the tin, refrigerate and then slice it into squares.

It keeps well in an air-tight container for 3 days in a cool place.

Macaron gone mad! Yes it is huge and is perfect for a summer party in much the same way that a Pavlova is a mountain of summer berries and whipped cream.

You could add a different food colour to each circle for a fun celebration. As long as your chosen fruit is light and not wet, the filling is firmly whipped and then it will all be perfect.

Serves 10
Wheat, gluten and
can be dairy-free

Strawberry
Macaron *Cake*

255g/9oz ground almonds

350g/2¾ cup icing/
confectioner's sugar

6 large free-range egg whites

Pinch of fine sea salt

150g/¾ cup caster/
superfine sugar

Filling
Plenty of good quality
strawberry jam

Plenty of whipped goat's double
cream/lactose-free cream or
dairy-free whipped soya cream

Lots of fresh, ripe, hulled,
quartered strawberries or
other mixed, whole, hulled red
berries (do not use frozen or
canned)

Optional: A dusting of icing/
confectioner's sugar

You will need to draw 3 x
23cm/9inch circles on baking
paper and line baking trays/
sheets with them.

Preheat the oven to 170ºC/150ºC fan/325ºF/Gas Mark 3.

Put the ground almonds and icing sugar into a bowl and stir to combine. In a separate bowl, whisk the egg whites and salt to soft peaks before adding the caster sugar, 2 tablespoons at a time, until thick and glossy.

Using a large metal spoon, fold the almond mixture into the egg whites. Spoon onto the lined baking sheets. Use a palette knife to smooth the circles. Tap each tray sharply on the work surface to level it off. Set aside for 15 minutes to form a slight skin. Bake the macarons for about 20 minutes or until crisp around the edges. Remove from the oven and cool.

Carefully remove each macaron from the baking sheet and place one on a large serving plate or cake stand. Spread plenty of jam lightly over the macaron. Whip plenty of cream and spread that over the jam. Use as much or as little as you like according to personal preference and expense of the ingredient. Top with a good scattering of strawberries. Top with the next macaron disk and repeat. Add the last macaron disk and top lightly with cream and fruit. Dust with extra icing sugar if you like. Serve or chill for a few hours but eat on the same day.

Using home-made fruit curd for this recipe is best and this time I am going to add the juice and zest of a lime to my lemon curd recipe, but you can use shop bought and do the same. It is gloriously tangy and feels like you have captured a jar of sunshine. Use organic eggs for the brightest of yellow preserves. Using a whisk helps keep the curd wonderfully light. The roulade freezes well, so you can make it well in advance for a party and take it out about 3 hours before it is needed. Unwrap the roulade when frozen onto a suitable serving plate. When it is defrosted decorate with a dusting of icing/confectioner's sugar.

Lemon & Lime Meringue Roulade

<u>Serves 6–8</u>
Wheat, gluten and
can be dairy-free

<u>Meringue Roulade</u>
*1 teaspoon pure cornflour/
cornstarch*

1 teaspoon pure vanilla extract

1 teaspoon white wine vinegar

4 large free-range egg whites

*150g/¾ cup caster/superfine
sugar*

*75g/scant ½ cup ground
almonds*

40g/1½oz flaked almonds

<u>Lemon and Lime curd</u>
<u>Makes 2 small jam jars</u>

*Zest and juice 3 large
unwaxed lemons and 1
unwaxed juicy lime*

*200g/1cup caster/
superfine sugar*

*100g/3½oz lactose-free/goat's
butter or dairy-free sunflower
spread*

*3 large free-range eggs and 1
extra egg yolk*

Line a 37 x 27cm (14½ x 10¾inch) silicone baking flexi-sheet or a traditional roulade tin which is slightly smaller, lined with non-stick paper or sheet.

Preheat the oven to 170°C/150°C fan/325°F/Gas Mark 3.

To make the meringue roulade, blend the first 3 ingredients to a smooth paste in a bowl.

In a large, dry metal bowl, whisk the egg whites until stiff peaks are formed using a hand-held electric whisk. Gradually whisk in the sugar only 2 teaspoons at a time and whisking well between each addition.

Using a metal spoon, gently fold in the cornflour mixture and then add the ground almonds into the meringue. Spoon the meringue over the prepared tin and gently level off the top and sprinkle liberally with the flaked almonds.

Bake in the oven for about 20–25 minutes when the meringue should be pale gold and dry and crisp to the touch. Remove from the oven and leave to cool.

Make the lemon and lime curd. Place a heatproof bowl over a pan of simmering water and ensure that the base of the bowl does not touch the water. Place all the zest and juice with the sugar and butter or spread and whisk from time to time until the butter or spread has melted. In a separate bowl mix all the eggs with a fork and then

Or use 300g/10oz jar top quality lime or lemon curd

Filling
175ml/1¼ cups lactose-free/ goat's double cream, whipped or whipped soya cream – or as much as you like!

Optional: Sifted icing/ confectioner's sugar and seasonal berries

whisk it lightly into the butter/spread mixture. The curd should be cooked in 15 minutes when it should be thick and heavy on the whisk. Remove from the heat and allow it to cool, stirring occasionally. Use what you need for the recipe and then transfer any left into a sterilized jar and seal. Store the curd for up to 2 weeks in the fridge.

Lay a sheet of non-stick paper on a dry and clean surface and carefully turn the meringue onto it. Peel off the non-stick lining paper.

Spread the cold curd all over the meringue. Stiffly whip up the cream and spread lightly over the curd. Roll up the meringue into a firm log shape using the non-stick paper or sheet underneath to guide you. It is fine that it cracks but carefully slide it onto your serving dish and chill before serving. Dust with icing sugar.

Lavender is abundant in gardens throughout the summer and it is precious not only for the oil it produces for scented soaps, for body or face products and soothing massage oils but also for culinary purposes and use in cordials. It is an aromatic herb – bees love it and so do butterflies. Fortunately, ants and deer hate the smell and so it is an effective organic deterrent.

Lavender *Meringues* & Pavlova

Serves 8
Wheat, gluten
and dairy-free

4 large free-range egg whites

225g/1cup ready-made lavender sugar or home-made (see below)

Optional: Pink food colouring

For Serving: Whipped lactose-free or goat's cream, or vanilla dairy-free ice cream or the ice cream recipes

Raspberry purée and whole raspberries

Mint leaves

You will need a large baking sheet lined with greaseproof paper or Teflon sheet.

To make your own lavender sugar: Mix a handful of dried lavender flowers into 1kg/2lb 2oz of unrefined caster/superfine sugar and store in jars with lids tightly sealed. Leave in a cool but not a damp or cold place for up to one year

Preheat the oven to 150ºC/130ºC fan/300ºF/Gas Mark 2.

To make the Pavlova draw a 23cm/9inch diameter circle on a piece of greaseproof paper and place it on the baking tray.

Take a large, clean and dry metal mixing bowl and whisk the egg whites until they reach soft peak. Use an electric hand whisk for speed. When you can turn the bowl upside down without the egg whites sliding out then they are perfect. Make sure that you do not over-beat the eggs or they will collapse. Whisk in a tablespoon of lavender sugar at a time and whisk after each addition until all the sugar is used up and the mixture is thick and glossy. If you are using pink food colouring you can drip in a few drops and swirl the colouring into the finished meringue mixture for a marbled look.

Spoon the mixture in piles over the circle of paper and then swirl the blobs with a blunt knife until they unite. Swish the meringue into high sides and a low flat base.

Turn the oven down to 140ºC/120ºC fan/250ºF/Gas Mark 1.

Bake the Pavlova for about 1½ hours until pale gold and crisp. Turn off the heat and leave the meringue in the oven for the night or the rest of the day. Peel off the paper and store the meringue for up to a week in an airtight container.

<u>For individual meringues</u>: Spoon 16 heaped tablespoons of the mixture around the prepared baking tray and bake, cool and store as above.

Fill the Pavlova with whipped cream or ice cream and serve with poached pears in winter or fresh berries in summer. I also love sliced peaches with nectarines piled on top and mango slices with passion fruit.

To serve the meringues simply fill with whipped cream or ice cream and serve with any fruit salad or poached fruit or just as a treat for afternoon tea. For dinner parties serve the meringues with drizzles of raspberry or any berry purée around the plate, a few fresh baby mint leaves and raspberries to decorate.

This is a traditional Danish Christmas recipe but we love it so much that we eat it throughout the winter. Every autumn, (usually from mid-September until around mid-November in North America and March through May in Chile and New Zealand), cranberries reach their peak of colour and flavour and are ready for harvesting from where they grow on long-running vines.

Festive *Rice Pudding* *with* Red *Wine* *Cranberry* Compote

Serves 6–8
Wheat, gluten and
can be dairy-free

Compote
500ml/2 cups good quality red wine

200g/1 cup caster/ superfine sugar

½ stick cinnamon

500g/1lb 2oz fresh or defrosted frozen cranberries

Rice pudding
300g/1½ cups pudding rice (short grain)

1.8 litres/3 pints full-fat lactose-free/goat's/sheep's milk or dairy-free unsweetened soya milk/sweetened coconut and almond milk

80g/heaped ⅓ cup caster/ superfine sugar

4 teaspoons pure vanilla extract

80g/3oz nibbed or flaked almonds, lightly toasted

400-500ml/16-20fl oz lightly whipped lactose-free/goat's cream or 2x cartons of whipped soya cream

Make the compote first: Stir the first 3 ingredients together in a pan over moderate heat until the sugar is dissolved. Add the cranberries and poach them gently in simmering liquid until tender. Remove the berries with a slotted spoon and transfer to a serving bowl. Reduce the wine until you have about 250ml/1 cup left and then pour it over the berries.

While the berries are cooking, make the rice pudding by putting the first 3 ingredients in a thick-based pan over moderate heat and bring to the boil. Reduce the heat to low and cook the rice until tender and the milk is absorbed. You can add more milk if necessary. Stir frequently so that nothing sticks to the base of the pan.

Stir in the vanilla extract and almonds, saving some for decoration.

When the rice is cooked allow it to cool and then fold in the whipped cream. Transfer to a serving bowl and either chill or serve at room temperature. Serve with warm berry compote drizzled over the top and a sprinkling of nuts. Very festive!

Blueberries are perennial bushes with indigo-coloured berries native to North America. The fruit is pale greenish at first, then reddish-purple, and finally dark purple when ripe, covered in a protective coating known as 'bloom'. They have a sweet taste when mature, with variable acidity. Blueberry bushes typically bear fruit in the middle of the growing season, so the peak of the crop can vary from May to August (in the northern hemisphere) depending upon the weather conditions.

Blueberry Bread Pudding

<u>Serves 6</u>
Wheat, gluten and can be dairy-free

1 loaf good quality gluten-free white sliced bread, crusts removed (I used both Antoinette Savill bread in UK and Vogel white bread in New Zealand)

500ml/2 cups fresh blueberries

750ml/3 cups lactose-free/ goat's/sheep's milk or dairy-free soya milk

200g/1cup caster/ superfine sugar

Good pinch cinnamon

2 teaspoons pure vanilla extract

6 large free-range eggs

Knobs of lactose-free/ goat's butter or dairy-free sunflower spread

You will need to soak the bread in milk for about 1 hour before baking.

Preheat the oven to 180ºC/160ºC fan/350ºF/Gas Mark 5.

Arrange the trimmed slices of bread neatly in a very deep oven-proof dish, I use one 30 x 20cm/12 x 8inch. For the finished dish, I used about 12 slices but it will depend on the size of your dish. A bigger and shallower dish will serve more people.

Sprinkle half the blueberries over the bread. Cover them with another layer of bread, trimmed to fit. Sprinkle with the remaining berries. Cover with a last layer of bread.

In a large mixing bowl, beat the milk, sugar, cinnamon, vanilla and eggs together. Pour the mixture over the layers of bread and leave to sit for an hour to absorb the liquid and flavours. Dot the top with plenty of little knobs of butter or spread and bake in the oven for about 1 hour or until a skewer inserted in the centre of the pudding comes out clean.

Serve hot.

Cakes, *Muffins,*
Cookies, Breads
& More

100g/3½oz sultanas

4 tablespoons water (rum, Cointreau or calvados can be used)

280g/2 cups My Gluten-Free Plain White Flour Blend (page 181)

1 teaspoon ground cinnamon

A good pinch of fine sea salt

1 teaspoon baking powder (check labels for allergens)

1½ teaspoons bicarbonate of soda/baking soda

125ml/½ cup light olive oil

160g/¾ cup caster/superfine sugar

½ vanilla pod, scraped out, keep seeds

2 large free-range eggs, lightly beaten

3 cooking apples, peeled, cored and cut into small dice

Zest 1 unwaxed lemon

2 large free-range egg whites

Maple Icing
100g/3½oz softened lactose-free/goat's butter or dairy-free sunflower spread

200g/1½ cups light muscovado sugar

85ml/⅓ cup maple syrup

255g/9oz lactose-free/goat's cream cheese, ricotta or dairy-free soya cream cheese-style spread or dip

You will need a 20cm/8inch spring-form cake tin, base and sides lined with baking parchment.

Olive oil gives this cake extra depth and intensity so it's worth keeping it for a day or two so that the flavours mature. Keep it in a cool place or in the fridge and it will certainly last a few more days too. You can just dust the cake with icing sugar for a less calorie-laden treat.

Apple & *Olive Oil* Cake *with* Maple Icing

Serves 6–8 • Wheat, gluten and can be dairy-free Ⓢ

Preheat the oven to 170ºC/150ºC fan/340ºF/Gas Mark 3.

Place the sultanas in water (or the alcohol if using) in a medium pan and simmer over low heat until all of the water has been absorbed. Leave to cool.

Sift together the flour, cinnamon, salt, baking powder and bicarbonate of soda and set to one side.

Put the oil, sugar and vanilla seeds in a bowl and whisk together and then gradually add the eggs. The mixture should be smooth and thick. Mix in the diced apples, sultanas and lemon zest and then lightly fold in the sifted dry ingredients.

Whisk the egg whites in a clean bowl with an electric hand whisk until firm peaks and fold into the batter as lightly as possible.

Pour the batter into the lined tin and level it off. Bake in the preheated oven for 1½ hours or until a skewer comes out clean. Remove from the oven and leave to cool in the tin.

Remove from the tin and place the cake on a plate or cake stand.

Make the icing by beating the first 3 ingredients together until light and airy with an electric hand whisk. Add the cream cheese and beat until the icing is smooth.

Use a palette knife to spread the icing all over the cake and create some fun wavy patterns or any pattern you like.

I serve this cake with the Lemon Curd Yogurt (page 176). It is a lovely contrast to the sweetness and intensity of the almonds and honey. Honey is expensive so you can drizzle as much or as little over the top of the cake as you like.

Serves 6–8
Wheat, gluten
and dairy-free

Almond Honey *Cake*

185g/6½oz ground almonds

4 large free-range eggs, separated

180ml/¾ cup clear honey, plus 2 tablespoons to serve

A pinch of fine sea salt

1 teaspoon pure vanilla extract

½ teaspoon baking powder (check label for allergens)

You will need a 23cm/9inch cake tin, greased.

Preheat the oven to 180ºC/160ºC fan/350ºF/Gas Mark 4.

Combine the ground almonds, egg yolks, honey, salt and vanilla until well mixed. Set aside. In a separate mixing bowl, whip the egg whites until very foamy but not forming peaks or stiff. Gently fold the egg whites into the honey mixture.

Sprinkle the baking powder over the mixture and combine gently. This should lessen the risk of the cake sinking in the middle. Pour the batter into the cake tin and gently tap the pan hard to knock out any air bubbles.

Bake in the oven for about 30 minutes or until golden brown and an inserted skewer comes out clean. Cool the cake and drizzle with honey before serving.

This is a fabulously easy cake to make and so delicious. All ages love the combination of creamy Nutella or dairy-free chocolate spread and cinnamon sponge. We take it on picnics in the summer and serve it with hot chocolate in the winter; perfect either way. It keeps for a week or you can freeze it in advance.

Serves 8
Wheat, gluten and
can be dairy-free

Chocolate & Hazelnut Swirl Cinnamon Cake

175g/6oz softened lactose-free/ goat's butter or dairy-free sunflower spread

175g/¾ cup caster/superfine sugar

3 large free-range eggs

200g/1½ cups self-raising flour blend

1 heaped teaspoon baking powder (check label for allergens)

2 teaspoons ground cinnamon

4 tablespoons full-fat lactose-free/goat's/sheep's milk or unsweetened soya milk

4 heaped tablespoons Nutella or dairy-free home-made Chocolate & Hazelnut Spread (page 173)

Cocoa powder (check label for allergens) and icing/ confectioner's sugar for dusting

You will need a lined non-stick 20cm/8inch round cake tin.

Preheat the oven to 180ºC/160ºC fan/ 350ºF/Gas Mark 4.

Put the first seven ingredients together in a big bowl and beat with an electric hand whisk for about 1 minute or until light and creamy.

Tip three quarters of the mixture into the prepared tin, lightly shake it level and then add 4 blobs of Nutella onto the mixture. Top with the remaining mixture, swirl a few times with a skewer and shake level again.

Bake in the oven for about 1 hour or until golden brown, firm to touch and springs back when lightly touched. Leave in the tin until cool, turn the cake onto a plate or onto a cake stand and dust with a mixture of sieved cocoa powder and icing sugar. Eat on the day or wrap and store for up to a week.

This is such a simple and delicious recipe. But it does need overnight soaking and long cooking. Using a good local ale would be nice but they are not gluten-free so I buy whatever gluten-free brand is available at my local supermarket. Not being a lager or ale aficionado these brands taste good to me.

Ale Fruit *Loaf*

Serves 8
Wheat, gluten
and dairy-free

400g/13½oz mixed dried vine fruit

250ml/1 cup gluten-free ale or lager

100g/¾ cup soft dark brown sugar

185g/1½ cup self-raising gluten-free plain white flour

3 teaspoons ground mixed spice

2 large free-range eggs, beaten

Standard non-stick loaf tin, greased and lined with non-stick baking paper.

Preheat the oven to 140ºC/120ºC fan/275ºF/Gas Mark 1.

Put the dried fruit into a large pan and cover with the ale or lager. Gently heat the fruit until the liquid is hot but not boiling. Remove from the heat, cover and leave overnight.

Add the sugar, flour, mixed spice and eggs to the fruit mixture. Combine the ingredients. Pour the mixture into the prepared tin. Bake in the preheated oven for 1¼ hours until risen, pale brown and firm to the touch. Cover with a tea towel and leave the loaf in the tin on a wire rack to cool. When the loaf is cold, wrap with cling film/plastic food wrap and store in a cool place for up to a month.

The better quality of tea you use the better the flavour of the loaf. This is very like the Irish fruit loaves that are so delicious and traditional.

This recipe is great for picnics and lunch boxes as well as afternoon tea in front of a roaring log fire. You can drizzle honey over the top if you like and this will give you a bit more sweetness and goodness. I recommend using a mild honey so that it doesn't overpower the loaf.

Apple Honey Tea *Loaf*

Serves 8
Wheat, gluten and
can be dairy-free
(S)

1 good quality tea bag steeped in 160ml/⅔ cup boiling water for 5 minutes and then discarded

150g/5oz sultanas

2 large free-range eggs, beaten

2 tablespoons runny honey

150g/1 heaped cup light muscovado sugar

225g/1½ cups My Gluten-Free Plain White Flour Blend (page 181)

2 heaped teaspoons baking powder (check label for allergens)

2 teaspoons mixed spice

2 large eating apples, peeled and cored

You will need a greased standard loaf tin, base-lined with baking parchment.

Preheat the oven to 180ºC/160ºC fan/350ºF/Gas Mark 4.

Pour the tea over the sultanas and leave to soak overnight.

Whisk the eggs, honey and sugar together in a large bowl until pale. Mix the flour, baking powder and spice together and fold into the egg mixture. Stir in the sultanas and liquid. Grate one and a half of the apples and stir into the cake mixture, then pour into the prepared loaf tin. Dice the remaining half apple into tiny pieces and scatter over the loaf. Bake for about 50–60 minutes or until cooked through.

I made these delicious brownies in secret one afternoon and as soon as they were ready they were fallen upon by my small daughter. As they were pronounced to be fabulous, I then admitted that they are made with beetroot! Too late to back-track, these brownies are now firm favourites. The beetroot gives an extra depth of flavour and consistency.

Red Velvet *Brownie Tray* Bake

Makes 12 or more
Wheat, gluten and
can be dairy-free

255g/9oz cooked whole
beetroot/beets or a pack
ready-cooked (no vinegar),
drained

200g/7oz dark chocolate,
70% cocoa solids (check
for allergens)

255g/9oz lactose-free/goat's
butter or dairy-free sunflower
spread

255g/1⅓ cups Demerara sugar

3 large free-range eggs

150g/1¼ cups My Gluten-Free
Plain White Flour Blend (page
181)

Line a 30cm x 20cm/12 x
9inch non-stick baking tin with
non-stick baking paper

Preheat the oven to 180ºC/160ºC fan/350ºF/Gas Mark 4.

Whiz the beetroot in a food processor until smooth.

Melt the chocolate and butter, or spread, in a bowl set over a pan of simmering water. Remove from the heat and stir gently until smooth.

In a bigger bowl whisk together the sugar and eggs until thick and pale in colour. Whisk in the melted chocolate, fold in the flour and then lightly fold in the beetroot purée. Pour the mixture into the prepared tin and bake for 20 minutes. Insert a skewer to test the brownies are cooked but there should be a bit of clingy mixture attached.

Leave to cool in the tin and when they are cold, cut them into 12 or more squares.

You can make any sort of topping you like; drizzle with melted chocolate, make chocolate ganache or icing or for contrast make the Cloud Nine Rose Cupcake cream cheese icing (page 148).

Sponge

225g/8oz lactose-free/goat's butter or dairy-free sunflower spread

100g/3½oz lavender sugar (blend a handful of lavender flowers in the liquidizer or food processor with caster/super-fine sugar until very fine and speckled with lavender)

125g/scant ¾ cup caster sugar/superfine sugar

Finely grated zest and juice of 3 unwaxed lemons

4 medium free-range eggs, beaten

225g/1 cup self-raising gluten-free white flour blend, sifted

Lemon Buttercream

Finely grated zest and juice of 2 large lemons

170g/6oz softened lactose-free/goat's butter or dairy-free sunflower spread

175g/1½ cup icing/confectioner's sugar, sifted

Icing

As much icing/confectioner's sugar as you like mixed with the remaining lemon juice from the buttercream

Decoration

Sugared primroses, mini Easter eggs are good for spring. A few sprigs of lavender in rafia string is fun in season or candles for a birthday

You will need two 20cm/8inch non-stick cake tins lined with non-stick baking paper.

This is the cake that I made for Richard's birthday this year and it was so delicious that everyone begged for the recipe. The sun-soaked scent of both lemons and lavender from pots on the veranda was delicious. Make a big batch of lavender sugar (page 126) and store it in a cool, dry place until needed.

Lemon & Lavender Cake

<u>Serves 8</u> • Wheat, gluten and can be dairy-free

Preheat oven to 190ºC/170ºC fan/375ºF/Gas Mark 5.

Cream the butter or spread with the sugars in a large bowl with an electric hand whisk or in a food processor until light and fluffy. Add all the lemon zest and then the eggs quarter at a time mixing briefly to keep the sponge light. Add a tablespoon of the flour if the mixture begins to curdle and combine briefly. Add the remaining flour as lightly as possible. Add the lemon juice and mix briefly.

Divide the mixture into the prepared tins and lightly spread and smooth the tops. Bake in the oven for about 20 minutes or until well risen, golden and springs back when lightly touched. Place the tins on a wire rack for 15 minutes, then turn cakes out onto a wire rack to cool. Don't forget to remove the baking paper.

Meanwhile, make the lemon buttercream by mixing all the lemon zest and half the juice, all the butter or spread and icing sugar together until light and creamy. You can use an electric hand whisk or food processor.

Place a cold sponge on a serving plate and spread all over with the buttercream. Place the remaining sponge on top.

Make up some very thick white icing for the top of the cake. Use as much or as little as you like depending on your intended decoration and sweet tooth. Simply beat the icing sugar with the remaining lemon juice until smooth and just spreadable.

Decorate to suit the occasion.

400g/3 cups gluten-free plain white flour

3 teaspoons baking powder (check labels for allergens)

2 teaspoons mixed spice

½ teaspoon fine sea salt

400g/3 cups soft dark brown sugar

3 large free-range eggs, lightly beaten

185ml/1¼ cup sunflower oil

225g/8oz peeled, deseeded and grated pumpkin or butternut squash

125ml/½ cup freshly squeezed orange juice

Maple Icing
100g/3½ oz softened lactose-free/goat's butter or dairy-free sunflower spread

200g/1½ cups light muscovado sugar

85ml/⅓ cup maple syrup

255g/9oz lactose-free/goat's cream cheese, ricotta or dairy-free soya cream cheese-style spread or dip

Decoration: Drizzle of runny honey and scattering of toasted flaked or nibbed almonds

You will need a 20 x 30cm/8 x 12inch tray-bake tin lined with non-stick baking paper.

The Celts traditionally put out food to placate angry spirits that roamed at Samhain, the end of the Gaelic calendar and in medieval times the poor went door to door on All Hallows' Eve offering prayers for the dead in return for something to eat. There are endless ideas for Halloween treats; tombstone cookies, haunted graveyard cakes and ginger biscuit bats. But sometimes all the cloying sweetness of endless candies and chocolates get a bit too much on the trick or treat run. So my pumpkin tray bake may be a bit rustic and homely but at least it is full of good things. We also eat it on Guy Fawkes Night with other staples like baked potatoes, sausages and soup as close to the bonfire as we can safely get.

Autumn Pumpkin Tray *Bake*

Makes about 20 squares • Wheat, gluten and dairy-free

Preheat the oven to 170°C/150°C fan/325°F/Gas Mark 3.

Put all the ingredients for the cake into a large mixing bowl and mix together until combined. Spoon the mixture into the prepared tin and bake in the preheated oven for about 50 minutes or until springy to touch. Cool the cake in the tin.

Meanwhile, make the icing by beating the first 3 ingredients together until light and airy with an electric hand whisk. Add the cream cheese and beat until the icing is smooth.

Use a palette knife to spread the icing all over the cake and create some fun wavy patterns or any pattern you like. Drizzle with honey and scatter with toasted flaked almonds.

Tip: it is handy to transport the cake in the tin but you can easily turn it out onto a clean tray and then decorate it.

This is such an easy cake to make and you can make it by hand if you do not have a food processor. It keeps for most of the week and so I make it mid-week for the weekend and keep it wrapped up in foil. It is also a marvellous Sunday lunch pudding served with a dollop of poached rhubarb and lots of custard.

Rhubarb &
Ginger Slice

Serves 6–8
Wheat, gluten and
can be dairy-free

300g/2¼ cups gluten-free self-raising white flour blend

2 teaspoons mixed spice

1 teaspoon ground ginger

140g/5oz lactose-free/goat's butter or dairy-free sunflower spread

100g/scant 1 cup dark muscovado sugar

255g/1 cup golden syrup

1 teaspoon bicarbonate of soda/baking soda

2 large free-range eggs, beaten

300g/10oz rhubarb, as pink and sweet as possible, cut into short lengths

You will need a greased 20cm/8inch square cake tin, lined with baking paper.

Preheat the oven to 180ºC/160ºC fan/ 350ºF/Gas Mark 4.

Sift the flour and spices into a mixing bowl.

In the food processor beat the butter or spread and sugar together until light and fluffy and then beat in the golden syrup.

Dissolve the bicarbonate of soda with 200ml/¾cup of boiling water in a small jug and gradually pour this down the spout of the processor, pulsing the mixture as you go along. Pulse in the flour mixture and then the eggs but keep it brief. Remove the blade and lift off the bowl from the processor and gently stir in the rhubarb.

Pour the mixture into the prepared tin and bake for about 50 minutes or until the cake top feels firm to touch and springs back when pressed. Cool in the tin and then turn out onto a wire rack until cold.

Swiss rolls are easy and quick to make as they don't have to be iced and can be filled with jam, buttercream, cream or even ice cream. To ring the changes I have filled mine with ricotta cheese or a dairy-free equivalent, home-made jam made from either quince or strawberries. We love Swiss roll as a dessert as well as a teatime treat.

Strawberry Swiss Roll

<u>Serves 6–8</u>
Wheat, gluten
and dairy-free

Sponge
3 large free-range eggs

85g/½ cup caster/superfine sugar, plus extra for dusting

1 teaspoon pure vanilla extract

1 tablespoon warm water

85g/heaped ½ cup gluten-free plain white flour

A pinch of salt

Filling

255g/9oz My Ricotta Cheese (page 185) or soft lactose-free/goat's/sheep's cream cheese or dairy-free soya cream cheese-style spread or dip

2 tablespoons icing/confectioner's sugar

1 teaspoon pure vanilla extract

255g/9oz ripe strawberries, hulled and finely sliced

Good quality or home-made strawberry jam

You will need a greased and lined Swiss roll tin. Non-stick baking paper or a Teflon sheet is even better.

Preheat the oven to 190ºC/170ºC fan/375ºF/Gas Mark 5.

Beat the eggs, sugar and vanilla in a large bowl with an electric hand whisk until the mixture is pale and mousse-like. Fold in the warm water with a large metal spoon. This should prevent the Swiss roll from cracking when you roll it. Use the metal spoon as lightly and briefly as possible so that you don't knock the air out of the mixture and lose the sponginess.

Sift and fold the flour into the mixture and then the salt. Pour the mixture into the prepared tin and level it off gently with a palette knife. Bake in the oven for about 10 minutes or until the sponge is firm to the touch and has shrunk back from the sides.

Remove from the oven and turn the Swiss roll out onto a sheet of baking paper sprinkled with a dusting of sugar. Leave to cool for 10 minutes and then gently peel off the lining paper from the sponge. Leave the sponge to cool completely.

In a bowl, mix the first 3 ingredients for the filling together until smooth and have your strawberries ready.

Trim the rough edges off the sponge with a sharp serrated knife. Spread a thin layer of the jam all over the sponge, cover with the filling mixture and then the sliced strawberries. If you have filling mixture left then you can use it with fresh berries or poached fruit.

contd. >

With the shortest side facing you, roll up the sponge away from you, using the paper to help you. The tighter you roll it, the more impressive the finished look. Carefully lift the Swiss roll onto a serving plate, placing it seam down so that it does not come undone. A good tip is to use a large fish slice or something like that, along with your hands to prevent accidental breakage. Sprinkle with a dusting of sugar and chill until needed.

At last, a recipe that doesn't use oats, holds together and tastes delicious. The date slices are packed with nutrients and the fresh dates impart the sweetness needed rather than excessive sugar.

Quinoa Date *Slices*

<u>Makes 16</u>
Wheat, gluten and
can be dairy-free

50g/⅓ cup gluten-free self-raising white flour blend

50g/⅓ cup My Gluten-Free Plain White Flour Blend (page 181)

100g/1 cup organic quinoa flakes

100g/3½ oz lactose-free/goat's butter or dairy-free sunflower spread

50g/½ cup soft brown sugar

200g/7oz fresh dates, stoned and chopped

2 tablespoons lemon juice

3 tablespoons hot water

You will need a 20cm/8inch square baking tin, lightly buttered.

Preheat the oven to 180ºC/160ºC fan/350ºF/Gas Mark 4.

Mix the flours and quinoa together, rub in the butter or spread and stir in the sugar to make a crumbly mix. Press half the crumb mixture into the bottom of the prepared tin.

Put the dates, lemon juice and hot water in a food processor and whizz until you have a thick, jam-like consistency that you can spread over the crumb base.

Firmly press the remaining crumbs over the date mixture and bake for 30 minutes. Cut into little squares whilst warm and leave to cool in the tin. Keep in the tin until they are cold.

<u>Tip</u>: only serve the date slices when they are cold or they will be crumbly.

Just the same sort of idea as carrot or courgette/zucchini cupcakes but we are not so used to using parsnips. The children didn't even notice the parsnips. I spread the delicious Maple Icing (page 132) in swirls over each one but you could make a chocolate, coffee or vanilla buttercream if you prefer.

Parsnip *Cupcakes* *With* Maple Icing

Makes 18 cupcakes
Wheat, gluten and
can be dairy-free
Ⓢ

Zest and juice 1 unwaxed lemon

115g/4oz parsnips, peeled and roughly grated

140g/5oz whole hazelnuts in their skins

30g/¼ cup My Gluten-Free Plain White Flour Blend (page 181), sifted

1 heaped teaspoon baking powder (check label for allergens)

A pinch of fine sea salt

1 heaped teaspoon ground cinnamon

30g/1oz walnuts, roughly chopped

3 free-range eggs, separated

100g/½ cup caster/superfine sugar

Maple Icing (page 132)

Arrange 18 paper cupcake cases in two bun trays.

Preheat the oven to 190ºC/ 170ºC fan/375ºF/Gas Mark 4.

Put the lemon zest in a large mixing bowl with 2 tablespoons of lemon juice. Mix the grated parsnips into the zest and set aside.

Put the hazelnuts and flour into a food processor and whiz until the nuts are finely ground. Add the baking powder, salt and cinnamon and whiz. Tip into the lemon zest bowl and mix in the walnuts.

In a large bowl, whisk the egg whites until they form soft peaks. Add 2 tablespoons of the sugar and continue to whisk, gradually adding the remaining sugar until it is all used up. You should have glossy peaks.

Roughly beat the egg yolks in a small bowl and using a metal spoon fold them into the egg whites. Fold in ⅓ of the flour mix and one third of the parsnip mix until all the ingredients are used up. Spoon into the paper cases and bake for about 15 minutes or until they are springy to the touch.

Cool the cupcakes on a wire rack. Chill the cupcakes for 2 hours so that they firm up. When they are firm you can ice them and serve them.

Make the icing and swirl as much or as little as you like on each cupcake.

Gloriously fudgy brownies go down well with every age-group and can be served with ice cream as a pudding, as treat for a cappuccino break or for afternoon tea. I cut the brownies into 16 adult-size pieces or 32 children's party-size pieces. You can of course replace the chopped-up dark chocolate with white chocolate and the cranberries can be replaced with dried cherries. For those who would rather have nuts exchange the dried fruit for your own choice of chopped nuts.

Makes 16
Wheat, gluten
and dairy-free

Double Chocolate & Cranberry *Brownies*

100g/3½oz dark chocolate, minimum 70% cocoa solids, broken into pieces (check for allergens)

115g/4oz lactose-free/goat's butter or dairy-free sunflower spread

200g/2 cups soft muscovado sugar

2 large free-range eggs, lightly beaten

110g/¾ cup white gluten-free plain flour blend

100g/3½oz dark, milk or white chocolate, chopped (depending on allergies)

75g/½ cup dried cranberries

You will need a deep-sided 20cm/8inch square baking tin, lined with non-stick paper or Teflon sheet.

Preheat the oven to 180ºC/160ºC fan/350ºF/Gas Mark 4.

Melt the chocolate pieces in a heatproof bowl set over a pan of simmering water. Make sure the bowl does not touch the water and stir the chocolate from time to time as it starts to melt. Once the chocolate has melted remove the bowl from the heat and stir until smooth.

Beat the butter or spread and sugar until light in a food processor or with an electric hand whisk in a bowl. Add the eggs a little at a time; keep on beating the mixture until you have used up all the beaten egg. Sift in the flour and briefly mix. Briefly mix in the melted chocolate and then very briefly fold in the chopped chocolate and cranberries.

Scrape the mixture into the tin and even it out gently. Bake the brownies in the oven for about 20 minutes or until just set. Leave to cool in the tin and then turn out onto a chopping board. Cut the brownies into squares and serve or store in an airtight container for 3–4 days.

I love to make these cupcakes from the late spring until December when my roses finally give up their heavenly blooms and retire for the winter. If you dip some rose petals in beaten egg white and sugar and dry them you can sprinkle them over the cupcakes for a lovely Mother's Day gift or afternoon tea. The strength of the rosewater varies so much so if you have an authentic Turkish or Middle Eastern brand then you might only need a teaspoonful.

Makes 12
Wheat, gluten
and dairy-free

Cloud Nine Rose *Cupcakes*

115g/4oz lactose-free/goat's butter or dairy-free sunflower spread

115g/⅔ cup caster/superfine sugar

2 large free-range eggs, lightly beaten

115g/¾ cup gluten-free self-raising white flour blend, sifted

1 tablespoon rose water

Icing
300g/10oz lactose-free/goat's cream cheese or My Ricotta Cheese (page 185), at room temperature or soya cream cheese-style spread or dip

85g/3oz lactose-free/goat's butter or dairy-free sunflower spread at room temperature

100g/scant 1 cup icing/confectioner's sugar, sifted

You will need a 12-hole non-stick muffin tray lined with 12 paper cases.

Preheat the oven at 180ºC/160ºC fan/350ºF/Gas Mark 4.

Cream together the butter or spread and sugar until pale and fluffy. Mix in the beaten eggs a little at a time. Use a large metal spoon to fold in half the flour and then the rose water and finally the remaining flour. Spoon the mixture into the cupcake cases. Bake for 16 minutes, or until a skewer inserted in the centre comes out clean. Remove from the oven and leave to cool.

Make the icing only once the cupcakes are cold.

In a bowl, beat the cream cheese until smooth and light using the lowest speed of an electric hand whisk or wooden spoon. In a separate bowl, beat the butter or spread and icing sugar together; start with a wooden spoon and once the icing sugar has blended in with the butter or spread use an electric mixer on the lowest setting. Alternatively, continue by hand, for at least 5 minutes. The mixture should turn almost white and become fluffy and light. Fold the cream cheese mixture into the butter or spread mixture and then use a spatula to sculpt a wavy topping on each cupcake. Decorate with edible purple or pink tones of glitter or with crystallized rose petals.

These are the most heavenly little cakes, light and moist but packed with flavour. You can use ripe plums, peaches or greengages in summer and ripe blackberries in the autumn.

<u>Makes 8</u>
Wheat, gluten
and dairy-free

Apricot Friands

125g/1 cup icing/confectioner's sugar, sifted

40g/⅓ cup My Gluten-Free Plain White Flour Blend (page 181)

100g/1 cup ground almonds

3 large free-range egg whites, whisked into soft peaks

100g/3½ oz lactose-free/goat's butter or dairy-free sunflower spread

3 large, ripe apricots, stoned and diced

3 tablespoons flaked almonds

You will need an 8-hole muffin tin lined with paper cases.

Preheat the oven to 200ºC/180ºC fan/400ºF/Gas Mark 6.

Put the icing sugar, flour and ground almonds into a large mixing bowl.

Fold the whisked egg whites and butter or spread into the dry ingredients. Gently mix in the chopped fruit. Spoon the mixture into 8 muffin cases in the tin. Sprinkle with the flaked almonds and bake for about 10 minutes or until springy to touch and golden to look at.

Allow the friands to cool before serving.

You can have fun with this recipe and change the herb to fresh thyme and the lemon zest to orange or even finely chopped lavender flowers and either of the citrus fruit zest.

Rosemary Shortbread

<u>Makes 12 cookies</u>
Wheat, gluten and
can be dairy-free

*55g/heaped ¼ cup caster/
superfine sugar and a little
extra for dusting*

*1 teaspoon finely chopped fresh
rosemary leaves*

*115g/4oz lactose-free/goat's
butter or dairy-free sunflower
spread*

*Finely grated zest of 1 large,
unwaxed lemon*

*170g/1¼ cups My Gluten-Free
Plain White Flour Blend (page
181), sifted*

*You will need lightly oiled
baking sheets.*

Preheat the oven to 180ºC/160ºC fan/350ºF/Gas Mark 4.

Put the sugar and rosemary in a food processor and whiz until finely chopped and blended. Add the butter or spread and the lemon zest, beat until pale and creamy. Beat in the flour until it comes together into solid dough. Scrape the dough out of the bowl and place on a flour-dusted clean surface. Lightly roll the dough to about 3-5mm/⅛-¼inch thick. Use the pastry cutter to cut out 12 cookies in all. You will have to re-roll the dough several times so be light and gentle with it.

Place the cookies on the prepared trays and prick several times with a fork. Bake for about 12 minutes until pale gold. Remove the shortbreads from the oven and dust with a little caster sugar. Leave them to cool and then carefully transfer to a wire rack.

This recipe uses a classic French beurre noisette, which literally means 'the colour of nuts', and is when butter is melted and cooked until just turning golden. This gives the madeleines a distinctive colour and nutty flavour.

Coffee & Chocolate Madeleines

Makes 12
Wheat, gluten and can be dairy-free

125g/4½oz lactose-free/goat's butter or sunflower dairy-free spread

100g/¾ cup icing/confectioner's sugar

30g/1oz ground almonds

30g/¼ cup My Gluten-Free Plain White Flour Blend (page 181)

1½ tablespoons cocoa powder (check labels for allergens)

A pinch of fine sea salt

½ tablespoon instant coffee granules

3 large, free-range egg whites

2 teaspoons local honey

1 teaspoon pure vanilla paste or extract

150g/5oz dark chocolate, (check for allergens) broken into pieces and melted in a bain-marie (a heatproof bowl set over a pan of simmering water)

You will need a 12-hole madeleine pan, greased and lightly floured or a rubber mould which is clean and dry.

Preheat the oven to 170ºC/150ºC fan/325ºF/Gas Mark 3.

Put the butter or spread into a saucepan over medium heat and allow to melt. Continue to cook until the butter turns golden brown. The spread will not do this. Remove from the heat and cool completely.

Sift the sugar, almonds, flour, cocoa powder and salt into a mixing bowl.

Whisk in the coffee granules, egg whites, honey and vanilla using a balloon whisk. Whisk in the cooled butter or spread.

Cover the bowl with cling film/plastic food wrap and refrigerate for 30 minutes. This helps to achieve the right texture. Spoon the mixture into the prepared madeleine pan or rubber mould. You can chill again for another 15 minutes which helps to make a firm skin when baked.

Bake the madeleines in the preheated oven for 10-15 minutes.

Allow to cool completely in the moulds and then gently turn them out onto a wire rack.

Melt the chocolate until smooth and glossy and cool slightly. Dip half of each madeleine into the chocolate so that one side is completely and thickly coated.

Allow the chocolate to set before serving.

Marshmallows are now very popular in the UK and there are lots of artisan companies making them. They are generally gluten-free which is a great treat and I have tasted some heavenly cloud-like marshmallows flavoured with real fruits and rose water and other such delights. You can buy lollipop sticks online, at some supermarkets or at Lakeland in the UK.

Marshmallow & *Chocolate* Pops

<u>Makes 20</u>
Wheat, gluten
and dairy-free

20 regular-sized marshmallows

100g/3½oz dark chocolate (minimum 70% cocoa solids), check for allergens

55g/2oz bashed-up gluten-free digestive biscuits (fine crumbs)

You will need 20 lollipop sticks.

Line a baking tray or sheet with baking parchment paper.

Push a stick into each marshmallow, standing them on the lined baking sheet.

Toast the marshmallows over a gas flame (adults only!) until they just start to caramelize. Return to the tray and do not attempt to lift them off the tray until set firm again.

Break the chocolate into pieces and melt in a bowl set over a pan of simmering water. Dip the marshmallows into the chocolate so that it comes up about ⅓ of the way up the marshmallow and dip into the biscuit crumbs. Return to the tray and leave to set. Eat or keep.

It seems to be the vogue to have muffins of epic proportions. I am not keen on this but if you prefer then do make 9 muffins instead of 12. These muffins are moist and light with a delicious cinnamon crunch on top.

Blackberry Crumble *Muffins*

Makes 12 • Wheat, gluten and can be dairy-free ⑤

Topping

1 heaped tablespoon gluten-free oats (old fashioned kind)

100g/½ cup caster/ superfine sugar

60g/½ cup My Gluten-Free Plain White Flour Blend (page 181)

2 teaspoons ground cinnamon

55g/2oz lactose-free/goat's butter or dairy-free sunflower spread

Muffins

200g/1½ cups My Gluten-Free Plain White Flour Blend (page 181)

150g/¾ cup sugar (any brown sugar)

½ teaspoon fine sea salt

2 teaspoons baking powder (check for allergens)

80ml/⅓ cup sunflower or light olive oil

80ml/⅓ cup lactose-free/goat's/ sheep's milk or dairy-free soya or almond and coconut milk

1 large free-range egg

Filling

2 small cartons fresh blackberries or pick your own in season

200g/7oz block of any suitable chocolate, chopped

You will need to line a muffin tray with 12 large paper muffin cases.

Preheat the oven to 200ºC/180ºC fan/400ºF/Gas Mark 6.

Make the crumble topping first by mixing all the ingredients together in a bowl with your fingertips. Leave to one side.

In a large bowl mix together the first 4 ingredients for the muffins and set aside.

In a jug mix the liquids with the egg. Mix the liquid mixture into the dry muffin mixture.

Fold in the blackberries, more or less is fine and then fold in as much of the chocolate as you fancy. You can just have the fruit and no chocolate in which case add more fruit. Do not over-mix or the fruit will become mushy.

Spoon the muffin mixture into the muffin cases and sprinkle with the crumble topping. Bake in the oven for about 20-25 minutes. Leave the muffins for an hour or until cold or they will be too crumbly.

Tip: do not use frozen or defrosted or even canned blackberries as they go mushy and make the muffins soggy and undercooked.

I love this recipe for melting moments and this filling works particularly well. You could use any curd as a filling, buttercream or just dip them into melted chocolate. They are very versatile and keep for ages in an air-tight container.

Makes 24
Wheat, gluten and
can be dairy-free

Passion Fruit
Melting Moments

255g/9oz lactose-free/goat's butter or dairy-free sunflower spread

1 teaspoon pure vanilla extract

80g/⅔ cup icing/ confectioner's sugar

255g/2 cups My Gluten-Free Plain White Flour Blend (page 181), plus extra for dusting

75g/½ cup cornflour/ cornstarch

4 ripe passion fruit

<u>Buttercream</u>
100g/3½oz lactose-free/goat's butter or dairy-free sunflower spread

115g/scant 1 cup icing/ confectioner's sugar

2 ripe passion fruit

You will need 3 baking trays lined with non-stick baking paper.

Preheat the oven to 150ºC/140ºC fan/300ºF/Gas Mark 2.

Beat the butter or spread, vanilla and sifted icing sugar with an electric hand whisk until pale. Stir in the combined sifted flour and cornflour in two batches. Remove the pulp from the passion fruit and stir into the mixture.

Roll the equivalent of 2 level teaspoons of the mixture into balls with floured hands. Place them about 2.5cm/1inch apart on the prepared trays. Dip a fork into a little extra flour and press the biscuits lightly.

Bake for about 15 minutes or until the biscuits are pale gold. Stand them on the trays for 15 minutes to cool before transferring to wire racks. While the biscuits cool, make the buttercream. Beat the butter or spread with the icing sugar until pale and fluffy. Beat in the passion fruit pulp. Sandwich the biscuits together, dust with a little extra sifted icing sugar. Store in the fridge until needed.

I love all these freeze-dried berries and powders, they are such fun and make everything taste zingy and alive. You can use any nut, any berry and any chocolate that suits you.

About 16 large cookies
Wheat, gluten and
can be dairy-free

Macadamia, Chocolate & Berry Cookies

200g/1½ cup My Gluten-Free Plain White Flour Blend (page 181)

1 teaspoon baking powder (check label for allergens)

Pinch of fine sea salt

170g/¾cup caster/ superfine sugar

100g/3½oz dark chocolate, chopped, at least 70% cocoa solids (check for allergens)

70g/2½oz macadamia nuts, chopped

7g/¼oz tub freeze-dried strawberries

110g/3½oz lactose-free/ goat's butter, melted

1 free-range egg, beaten

You will need a couple of greased non-stick baking sheets.

Preheat the oven to 180ºC/160ºC fan/350ºF/Gas Mark 4.

Sift the flour into a bowl with the baking powder and the salt. Stir in the sugar, chocolate, nuts and strawberries. Add the cooled melted butter or spread and the egg. Mix to a soft dough. Turn onto a lightly floured surface and knead lightly into a sausage shape 5cm/2inch in diameter. Wrap tightly in baking parchment using the paper to shape a neat roll, twisting the ends to seal. Wrap in foil and store in the fridge or freezer until needed.

If frozen remove the cookie mix from the freezer for about 5 minutes before slicing. Cut off thin slices and place on the prepared baking sheets with room to spread. Bake for 10-12 minutes until pale golden. Cool on the tray for 5 minutes then transfer to cooling racks until cold.

This is a classic recipe which I have changed so that you can have it for a treat with ice cream or simply with coffee or tea. My recipe is quite gingery but you can add more or less ginger according to taste. They keep for ages in a tin or sealed container. The icing takes a bit of time to combine so I use a balloon whisk to help it blend together but don't be tempted to use it until it is smooth and glossy.

Ginger Crunch

<u>Makes about 20</u>
Wheat, gluten and
can be dairy-free

<u>Base</u>
175g/6oz lactose-free/goat's butter or dairy-free sunflower spread

140g/¾ cup caster/superfine sugar

175g/1¼ cup My Gluten-Free Plain White Flour Blend (page 181)

2 teaspoons ground ginger

1½ teaspoons baking powder (check label for allergens)

<u>Icing</u>
100g/3½oz lactose-free/goat's butter or dairy-free sunflower spread

125g/1 cup icing/confectioner's sugar

2 tablespoons golden syrup

4 teaspoons ground ginger

You will need to grease and line a 25cm x 20cm/10 x 8inch baking tin.

Preheat the oven to 190°C/170°C fan /375°F/Gas Mark 5.

Cream the butter or spread with the sugar until pale. Sift the flour, ginger and baking powder and mix until combined. Press evenly into the tin.

Bake for about 25 minutes until it is firm to touch. Remove from the oven and gently level out the base with the back of a wooden spoon. Ice while the base is still warm.

Heat the icing ingredients in a small saucepan. Stir until melted and combined. Pour the icing over the warm base and spread out evenly. Pop it into the deep freeze to chill as quickly as possible. Once the icing is set, cut the ginger crunches into squares using a hot, wet knife.

Store in an air-tight container in a cool place or keep in the fridge.

These little treasures are delicious with most desserts and ice creams or simply served with a cup of tea, coffee or a mug of steaming hot chocolate. I have never made Florentines without a chocolate backing but these work so extremely well that I am hooked.

Almond & Orange Florentines

<u>Makes about 20</u>
Wheat, gluten
and dairy-free

2 free-range egg whites

100g/¾ cup unrefined icing/ confectioner's sugar

255g/9oz flaked almonds

Grated zest 1 unwaxed orange

Vegetable oil for brushing

Preheat the oven to 150ºC/130ºC fan/300ºF/Gas Mark 2.

Line a heavy baking tray with baking parchment and brush lightly with vegetable oil. Have ready a small bowl of cold water.

Put the egg whites, icing sugar, flaked almonds and orange zest in a bowl and gently mix them together. Dip your hand in the bowl of water and pick up portions of the mix to make little mounds on the lined tray, well spaced apart. Dip a fork in the water and flatten each biscuit so they are very thin. Try to make them as thin as possible without creating too many gaps between the almond flakes. They should be about 8cm/3inch diameter.

Place the baking tray in the centre of the oven and bake for about 12 minutes, until the biscuits are golden brown. Check underneath one biscuit to make sure they are cooked through.

Allow to cool, and then gently, using a palette knife, remove the biscuits from the baking sheet. Store them in a sealed jar.

Base

270g/2 cups My Gluten-Free Plain White Flour Blend (page 181)

135g/1 cup gluten-free self-raising white flour blend

75g/1 cup desiccated/shredded coconut

400g/2 cups brown sugar

275g/3 cups gluten-free rolled oats (the old-fashioned kind)

2 large free-range eggs

300g/10oz lactose-free/goat's butter or dairy-free sunflower spread

Filling

200g/7oz lactose-free/goat's butter or dairy-free sunflower spread

340g/12oz can of Soymilke Dulce de Leche flavour or about 400g/12oz Confiture de Lait (page 172)

4 tablespoons golden syrup

2 teaspoons pure vanilla extract

You will need a greased 30 x 20cm/12 x 8inch deep tin lined with non-stick baking paper. Make sure the paper has a good overhang.

Although it is easy to make and quick, this recipe is at its best when left overnight to chill or whack them into the deep-freeze until firm but make sure they don't actually freeze. The crunchies will cut into firm and neat slices and taste even more luscious. I am rather addicted to Dulce de Leche and any excuse to create a recipe with this magic ingredient is a vote winner for a teatime treat. It is sometimes made with sweetened condensed milk which is not dairy-free but delicious too.

Caramel Oat Crunchies

Makes 8–10 • Wheat, gluten and dairy-free

Preheat the oven to 180ºC/160ºC fan/350ºF/Gas Mark 4.

Make the base: Combine the dry ingredients in a mixing bowl. Add the eggs and butter or spread. Mix well, then press two-thirds of the mixture into the prepared tin.

For the filling: Melt the butter or spread slowly with the Dulce de Leche and golden syrup. Mix well and add the vanilla extract. Pour onto the base. Sprinkle with the remaining crumbled mixture. Bake for about 30 minutes. Cool in the tin and chill overnight in the fridge. Cut into slices and serve. Keep these goodies cool.

Nice and easy which makes them child-friendly for weekend baking. I am not a great fan of coconut but in this recipe it is rather good.

I make this often as not with damson jam/jelly, blackcurrant or blackberry jam/jelly. Black cherry would be delicious too but anything bland wouldn't work.

<u>Makes about 16</u>
Gluten, wheat
and dairy-free

New Homestead Raspberry *Slices*

<u>Cake</u>
150g/5oz softened lactose-free/goat's butter or dairy-free sunflower spread

55g/¼ cup caster/superfine sugar

2 large free-range egg yolks

270g/2 cups gluten-free self-raising white flour blend, sifted

200g/¾ cup raspberry jam or more if you like

<u>Meringue</u>
2 large free-range egg whites

115g/½ cup caster/superfine sugar

115g/1½ cups desiccated/shredded coconut

You will need a greased 30 x 20cm/12 x 8inch Swiss roll tin lined with non-stick baking paper. Make sure the paper has a good overhang.

Preheat the oven to 180ºC/160ºC fan/350ºF/Gas Mark 4.

Cream the butter or spread and sugar together until light and fluffy, then add the egg yolks and beat until well combined. Stir in the flour and use your hands to achieve an even consistency. Press the mixture into the prepared tin and spread the jam all over it.

To make the meringue beat the egg whites and sugar until thick, then fold in the coconut. Spread the meringue over the top of the jam so that it is evenly covered.

Bake for about 20–25 minutes and cool in the tin before serving. The slice must be cold so that it cuts easily and doesn't crumble.

This soda bread is light and ideal for eating with soups, salads and savoury snacks or meals. If you don't have any sage then you can use thyme or chopped chives. Eat warm on the day of baking.

Cheese & Sage White Gluten-Free Soda Bread

Makes 1 loaf
Wheat, gluten-free
and can be lactose-free

200g/1½ cups My Gluten-Free Plain White Flour Blend (page 181)

1 heaped teaspoon bicarbonate of soda/baking soda

Large pinch fine sea salt

100g/1½ cups grated hard lactose-free semi-hard or goat's/sheep's milk hard cheese

 A large handful fresh sage leaves, chopped

250ml/1 cup plain lactose-free/goat's milk yogurt

You will need a small non-stick baking tray.

Preheat the oven to 200ºC/180ºC fan/400ºF/Gas Mark 6.

Put the flour, bicarbonate of soda and salt into a medium-sized mixing bowl. Mix in the grated cheese and sage leaves. Use a blunt-ended knife to mix in the yogurt and mix to a soft dough. Knead briefly until smooth. Gather the ball of dough and place it on the baking tray. Flatten the dough just enough with a gentle touch of the palm of your hand so that you can score a cross in the top with a sharp knife.

Bake in the oven for 25 minutes and double check that the bread is done by tapping the base which should sound hollow.

Rather like cornbread this recipe has a more cakey texture and taste than our usual soda breads and is a great last-minute alternative if you run out of bread. Vary the dried fruits to mixed peel and sultanas or raisins and currants for a change.

American Raisin Soda *Bread*

Makes 1 loaf
Wheat, gluten and
can be dairy-free

320g/2 cups My Gluten-Free Plain White Flour Blend (page 181) or bread flour blend

2 tablespoons caster/superfine sugar

1 heaped tablespoon baking powder (check labels for allergens)

1 teaspoon bicarbonate of soda/baking soda

¾ teaspoon fine sea salt

85g/½ cup lactose-free/goat's butter or dairy-free sunflower spread

85g/½ cup raisins or mixed dried vine fruits and citrus peel

175ml/¾ cup plain lactose-free/goat's/sheep's yogurt or dairy-free plain set soya yogurt

You will need a baking tray lined with a sheet of flour-dusted, non-stick paper or Teflon sheet.

Preheat the oven to 230ºC/210ºC fan/450ºF/Gas Mark 8. Please allow for oven temperature differences and adjust it to 220ºC/200ºC fan/425ºF/Gas Mark 7 if your oven temperature is slightly unstable.

Combine the first 5 ingredients in a large bowl. Cut in the butter or spread with a blunt knife to make small crumbs. Mix in the raisins, add the yogurt and mix in. Turn the dough onto the prepared tray and knead very gently and very briefly with your flour-dusted hands until it comes into a ball shape. Flatten the dough into an 18cm/7inch circle and score an X with a sharp knife.

Bake for about 20–25 minutes until dark golden brown. You can carefully test that the bread is cooked through by tapping the top and it should sound fairly hollow.

Fabulous to have gluten-free flatbreads at last. They transform Indian meals, hot and cold dips and warm salads. They are easy to make and suit most people as they don't have yeast in them.

Speedy Seeded *Flatbreads*

Makes 8
Wheat, gluten
and dairy-free

100g/¾ cup gluten-free self-raising white flour blend, plus extra for dusting

100g/¾ cup buckwheat flour

4 level teaspoons baking powder (check label for allergens)

½ teaspoon fine sea salt

3 heaped tablespoons mixed seeds (sesame, sunflower, rapeseed and flaxseed)

250ml/1 cup plain set Greek-style lactose-free/sheep's/goat's yogurt or dairy-free soya plain set yogurt

You will need a large non-stick baking sheet very lightly dusted with flour.

Heat the grill until very hot. Sift the flours into a mixing bowl, add the baking powder, salt and seeds. Stir in the yogurt to make a soft dough.

Gently divide the dough into 8 equal pieces, then very lightly roll and pat each one into an oval with floured hands. Place them on the prepared baking sheets. Grill them for about 3 minutes on each side or until golden brown and slightly puffed. Keep warm and eat as soon as possible.

This bread is rather moreish. I have it with soups and salads but also have it with My Ricotta Cheese (page 185). Depending on the flour blend that you use, you may have to increase the yogurt or it could be too light and crumbly. But in any case you must not be tempted to slice the bread until it is stone cold or it will definitely be too crumbly. This bread is designed to be eaten on its own without any butter or spread.

American Zucchini Bread

Makes 1 large loaf
Wheat, gluten and can be dairy-free

Ⓢ

270g/2 cups My Gluten-Free Plain White Flour Blend (page 181)

3 teaspoons baking powder (check label for allergens)

1 teaspoon bicarbonate of soda/baking soda

½ teaspoon cinnamon

A good sprinkling of each: paprika, coriander and cumin powder

½ teaspoon fine sea salt

85g/½ cup brown sugar

175ml/¾ cup melted, cooled lactose-free/goat's butter or dairy-free sunflower spread

2 large free-range eggs

1 teaspoon vanilla extract

Juice and zest 1 large lemon

2 small courgettes, grated /1 cup grated zucchini

125g/½ cup plain lactose-free/goat's yogurt or dairy-free plain soya yogurt

You will need a lined non-stick, large 25 x 14cm/10 x 5½ inch loaf tin/pan.

Preheat the oven to 200ºC/180ºC fan/400ºF/Gas Mark 6.

In a large bowl combine the flour, baking powder, bicarbonate of soda, spices and salt.

In another bowl, beat the sugar and melted butter or spread together. Add the egg, vanilla, lemon juice and zest, grated courgette and lastly the yogurt.

Stir the dry ingredients into the wet ingredients, do not over-mix.

Spoon the batter into the prepared loaf tin and level off. Bake in the preheated oven for about 50 minutes or until an inserted skewer comes out clean.

Remove from the oven and leave in the tin until cold. Turn the bread out and slice or store for up to 12 hours in a sealed container.

It is not easy to find allergy-free sponge fingers and so these are invaluable for Tiramisu recipes, chocolate mousse terrines and trifles. If you have toddlers with allergies then these are great for teatime treats.

Sponge *Fingers*

2 large free-range eggs, separated

100g/½ cup caster/superfine sugar

100g/¾ cup My Gluten-Free Plain White Flour Blend (page 181)

½ teaspoon baking powder (check label for allergens)

You will need 2 large non-stick baking trays lined with non-stick baking paper and piping bag with a plain round tube.

Preheat the oven to 200°C/180°C fan/400°F/Gas Mark 6.

Place the egg whites in a bowl and beat on high until soft peaks form. Slowly add 2 tablespoons of the sugar. Continue beating until the mixture is stiff and glossy. In another bowl beat the egg yolks with the remaining sugar until thick and very pale in colour.

Fold half the egg whites into the egg yolk mixture and then sift the flour and baking powder into the egg yolk mixture, folding them in gently. Fold in the remaining egg whites and then transfer the mixture into the piping bag.

Pipe out fingers, 8cm/3 inches long, keeping them apart so that they do not expand into each other. Bake in the preheated oven for 8 minutes. They will be pale gold and slightly puffy. Leave to cool on the paper and then lift them carefully onto a wire rack. Use them in a recipe on the same day.

These cookies are child's-play to make and provide a healthier snack than some cookies. I often use dried blueberries and walnuts for this recipe to bring in the changes for packed lunches and weekend nibbling.

Makes 16
Wheat, gluten
and dairy-free

Giant Oatmeal *Cookies*

130g/4½oz lactose-free/goat's butter or dairy-free sunflower spread

185g/1 cup brown sugar

60ml/¼ cup local honey

1 large free-range egg

1 teaspoon pure vanilla extract

Zest of 1 unwaxed orange

110g/¾ cup My Gluten-Free Plain White Flour Blend (page 181)

½ teaspoon fine sea salt

Heaped ½ teaspoon bicarbonate of soda/baking soda

255g/3 cups gluten-free (old-fashioned large) oats

180g /1½ cups dried cranberries

115g/4oz chopped pecans

You will need two non-stick baking trays lined with non-stick paper or Teflon sheets.

Preheat the oven to 180°C/160°C fan/350°F/Gas Mark 4.

Cream the butter or spread with the sugar and honey in a large bowl with an electric mixer or electric hand whisk. Add the egg, vanilla and orange zest and beat until light and creamy.

In a separate bowl, mix the flour, salt and bicarbonate of soda and stir into the butter mixture. Add oats, cranberries and pecans and combine together. Scoop out about 16 balls of the mixture, arrange them, well spaced on the prepared trays. Use wet hands to flatten each one so that they are thick and round. Bake for about 14–16 minutes until dark golden brown and firm looking.

If you want smaller cookies, simply reduce the cooking time to 10–12 minutes.

Confiture de lait or 'milk jam' is similar to the well-known Dulce de Leche but in Normandy it is made from whole milk and not condensed milk. It is eaten in Normandy on bread or toast, as a topping for pancakes or ice cream. It is a heavenly concoction and I have to ration it. I have used this recipe to make a filling for the macarons (page 118), Caramel Meringue Slice (page 121), Caramel Oat Crunchies (page 162) and a filling for Buckwheat Pancakes (page 120) but it is a great gift for friends any time of the year. The jam will keep for several months in the sealed jars in the fridge.

Makes 4 small jars (about 150g/5oz each)
Wheat, gluten and can be dairy-free

(s)

1 litre/1¾ pints lactose-free whole milk/goat's/sheep's milk

500g/1lb 1oz granulated sugar or Demerara sugar for the other milks

1 whole vanilla pod, split open or 1 teaspoon vanilla paste

Confiture *De Lait*

Pour the milk into a large thick-based pan and add the sugar and vanilla pod or paste. Bring the mixture to the boil over moderate heat and then reduce the heat so that you have a constant simmer. For this quantity, cook for about 3 hours stirring every 10–15 minutes. If you are making double the quantity, it will take about 5 hours. Either way, you need an alarm for this or you might forget and the jam might catch on the bottom or the sides of the pan. I make it when I am working in my office or we are all in the kitchen doing activities. As the mixture reduces the simmer bubbling increases and that is fine.

Sterlize your jars in good time.

When the mixture is golden caramel colour and thickens, remove the vanilla pod. The jam is ready when it is thick somewhere between a soft honey or Nutella. Fill the sterilized jars, seal and turn them upside down. Once they are cool, transfer the jars to a cool place and store for 2–3 days before eating or refrigerate for up to 6 weeks.

If you cannot eat Nutella due to the dairy content then this is perfect for spreading on warm bread, toast or using in cakes and cookies. I sandwich together shortbread biscuits or I make Chocolate & Hazelnut Swirl Cinnamon Cake (page 134). I like to give a jar of it as a gift to friends and they can store it for 3 weeks in the refrigerator before using.

Home-made *Chocolate & Hazelnut* Spread

Fills one medium-sized jam jar
Wheat, gluten and dairy-free

125g/1 cup hazelnuts, roasted and peeled

60g/½ cup icing/confectioner's sugar

55g/⅔ cup unsweetened cocoa powder (check for allergens)

2 teaspoons vanilla paste or pure vanilla extract or more if you prefer

A pinch fine sea salt

4 tablespoons melted coconut oil

Put the prepared hazelnuts into a food processor and blend until they have formed a smooth paste. This may take a couple of minutes. Scrape down the sides of the bowl as needed throughout the recipe. Add all the other ingredients and process until smooth, it takes about 5 minutes or so.

Transfer the spread to the jar, seal and store until needed. Keep it at room temperature for easy spreading.

This is my cheating chutney recipe and it is perfect with game and meat terrines, cheeses and salads and of course leftover cold Sunday roast meat or chicken. Anyone with a glut of pears will be thrilled with this recipe as pears are notoriously hard to freeze and a bit of a bother to bottle. If you keep the quantities small as in the recipe, you will find it cooks very quickly.

Makes 1x450g/1lb jar
Wheat, gluten
and dairy-free

Speedy Pear *Chutney*

2 red onions, halved and
finely sliced

2 tablespoons olive oil

1 teaspoon ground allspice

1 teaspoon mixed spice

1 teaspoon ground ginger

2 tablespoons unrefined dark
muscovado sugar or natural
molasses sugar

4 large unripe pears, peeled,
cored and diced

4 tablespoons sultanas

4 tablespoons redcurrant,
quince or crab apple jelly

2 tablespoons balsamic vinegar

2 tablespoons cider vinegar

Freshly ground black pepper
and grated nutmeg

You will need 1 x 450g/1lb
warm, sterilized jam or Kilner
(glass) jar for the chutney, with
some spare to eat on the day or
use a couple of smaller jars.

Make the chutney by cooking the onions in the oil over moderate heat until softened but not browned. Add the rest of the ingredients and cook until the pears are tender and the chutney is syrupy. Stir as little as possible so as not to break up the pears and don't let it dissolve into mush. Fill the prepared jar or jars with chutney, seal and leave to cool before storing in the fridge until needed.

I use this luscious mix as an accompaniment to various cakes and poached seasonal fruits. It is also yummy with pancakes and berries for breakfast or with baked seasonal fruits, both of which give you the contrast of hot and cold.

Serves 6–8
Wheat, gluten and
can be dairy-free

Lemon Curd *Yogurt*

450g/1lb set Greek sheep's
yogurt/goat's yogurt/
lactose-free yogurt or
dairy-free soya yogurt

225g/8oz good quality
lemon curd or make your
own lemon curd

Zest of 1 unwaxed lemon

Lightly combine the ingredients in a serving bowl, cover and chill until needed. The mixture should be streaked with curd rather than a uniform colour or texture.

Passion fruit has just enough acidity to make a delicious curd but it is gentle and sophisticated unlike the sharp lemon curd that we know and cherish. This passion fruit curd is excellent as a filling for meringues, macarons, petits fours, cakes and biscuits. See the recipes on pages 90 and 102.

Passion Fruit Curd

Makes 2 jars
Wheat, gluten and
can be dairy-free

12 large ripe passion fruit, halved

4 large free-range eggs

175g/scant 1 cup caster/ superfine sugar

115g/4oz lactose-free/goat's butter or dairy-free sunflower spread

You will need 2 sterilized 450g/1lb jam jars with lids

Squeeze the passion fruit into a sieve and push the pulp through to extract about 125ml/½ cup of juice. Reserve the seeds. Set a heatproof bowl over a pan of simmering water.

Combine the 3 eggs and one egg yolk with the pulp in the bowl and then whisk until warm. Add the sugar and the butter and briefly whisk again.

Use a wooden spoon to stir the mixture over gentle heat for about 20 minutes or until the mixture coats the back of the spoon. Stir in the seeds.

Pop the warm curd into the prepared jars and top with a round of greaseproof paper brushed in brandy. Seal and store in the fridge for up to 4 weeks. Any leftover curd can be spread on scones or toast and eaten fresh on the day.

Tip: always serve the curd cold or chilled or it will be runny.

This is a delicious recipe for fudge and you can have fun and play around with flavours. Add 2 teaspoons of brandy or Cointreau rather than vanilla extract for a special gift and you can replace ½ cup of white sugar with soft brown sugar. Keep the fudge in a cool place until you gift wrap it. You can serve the fudge with coffee or hot chocolate after a lunch or dinner. I like to finely chop some of the fudge pieces and sprinkle it over scoops of vanilla, coffee and chocolate dairy-free ice cream. Totally divine!

<u>Serves 8</u>
Wheat, gluten
and dairy-free

Chocolate Fudge

625g/3 cups white granulated sugar

55g/⅔ cup cocoa powder (check that it is dairy-free)

A large pinch of fine sea salt flakes

400ml/14oz tin full fat coconut milk

45g/¼ cup dairy-free sunflower or olive oil spread

2 teaspoons pure vanilla extract

You will need a thermometer and a big saucepan.

Line 20cm/8inch square baking tin or dish with aluminium foil, allowing the foil to hang over the sides as you will need this to lift the fudge out of the dish. Lightly oil the foil with a tasteless oil, I use extra light olive oil.

Combine the sugar, cocoa, salt and coconut milk in the pan. Stir over medium heat until the sugar dissolves and the mixture comes to a full boil. Boil the mixture, not stirring, until the temperature reaches 234°C or soft ball stage on your thermometer.

Remove the pan from the heat and add the chosen spread and the vanilla. Let the bubbling subside and then beat vigorously with a wooden spoon.

The mixture will become thick as it cools and will lose its gloss. Quickly pour and scrape the fudge into the prepared tin and set aside to cool. Carefully lift the cold fudge out of the tin using the foil lining. Cut into squares and serve.

Master
Recipes

This is the first time that I have made my own flour blend and I have found it fabulous. This blend produces baked goods and sauces with a perfect texture, colour and flavour and has definitely improved the overall recipes and end products. I have chosen these particular flours for two reasons; one, that they are the least expensive of the flours on offer and secondly the end results are light in taste, texture and colour. I generally make up quadruple quantities of this recipe and store it in an air-tight container to keep it fresh and to have it on hand for impromptu baking and cooking. All my flours are organic but that is just my preference and not necessary.

My Gluten-Free *Plain White Flour* Blend

1 batch or multiply this mix by as many times as you like
Wheat, gluten and can be dairy-free

100g/¾ cup/3½oz white rice flour

55g/½ cup/2oz potato flour

25g/¼ cup/1oz cornflour/ cornstarch

55g/scant ½ cup/2oz buckwheat flour

Mix all the ingredients in the given order. Store in a cool place and use within the stated date on the packets.

Please note that all these alternative flour weights and cup measures are different from standard wheat, plain or self-raising flour. I have measured and tested the recipes in grams and confirmed in cups. Cup measurements may vary slightly depending on the flour you use.

This is my recipe that has been successfully used in every cookbook that I have written. You can use any sort of butter or the dairy-free spreads that are now readily available. If you use butter, you will have a richer pastry that is easier to handle and lighter in texture. You can use all butter if you do not want to use hard white vegetable shortening for any reason. As with all pastry, keep it cool, handle it lightly and chill before baking. Always add the water even if you think the dough looks all right without it as it will not roll properly if it is too dry. As this recipe can be used in any other of your own favourite recipes I have listed metric, imperial and cup measures.

Serves 6–8
Wheat, gluten and
can be dairy-free
Ⓢ

My Gluten-Free *Shortcrust* Pastry

225g/1¾ cup/8oz My Gluten-Free Plain White Flour Blend (page 181)

A pinch of fine sea salt

55g/⅓ cup/2oz lactose-free/goat's butter or dairy-free sunflower spread

55g/⅓ cup/2oz hard white vegetable shortening (Trex and Cookeen are good)

1 large free-range egg, beaten

2 tablespoons cold water or more if necessary

You will need a 23cm/9inch round, loose-bottomed fluted metal tin for the best results or one or two 12 deep bun hole tin for tartlets. You will need baking paper and ceramic balls if baking pastry shells blind.

Preheat the oven to 180ºC/160ºC fan/375ºF/Gas Mark 4.

Hold the sieve as high as possible and sift the flour and salt into a large mixing bowl. Add the butter or sunflower spread and cut the remaining fat into small cubes and mix both into the flour with a blunt knife and then with your floured fingertips.

Keep your hands as high as possible to aerate the mixture. When the mixture resembles breadcrumbs, add the beaten egg and sprinkle with water. The dough will not roll out without sticking if it is too wet; equally it will break up if too dry. Mix with the knife until the pastry comes together into a smooth ball of dough and leaves the sides of the bowl fairly clean.

Flour a clean surface on your kitchen worktop. Place the dough in the centre of the floured area and flour your rolling pin.

Roll the dough into a large enough circle to line the tin. Gently guide the pastry over the tin and line it. If it breaks up a bit then simply mend and blend with your fingers until it looks smooth and even. It will still bake up nicely. Gently press the pastry into the flutes as high as

contd. >

you can, if it rises above the tin all the better as this will help prevent too much shrinkage. Lightly trim off any excess pastry from around the dish and prick the base with a fork. Put it in the deep-freeze for 10 minutes.

 If you are making tartlets then roll the dough out more thinly into a very big circle. The pastry needs to be thinner or the tartlets will be overwhelmed by the pastry. Cut out 12–18 circles with a metal pastry cutter. You can re-roll the pastry 2 or 3 times if your original roll is not sufficient.

Line the tins with the pastry and chill in the deep-freeze for 10 minutes. Excess tartlets can be frozen at this point for future baking.

For both: Line the pastry shell or shells with non-stick baking paper and a heap of ceramic balls and bake blind in the centre of the hot oven for about 25 minutes for the tart and 15 minutes for the tartlets.

Carefully remove the paper and hot ceramic balls, return the pastry case or cases to the oven and bake for a further 10 minutes for the tart and 5 minutes for the tartlets, or until golden and the base is cooked through. This is now perfect if no further baking is needed for the desired filling. If you are going to fill the pastry shell or shells and bake further, reduce the first cooking by 5 minutes and then remove the paper and ceramic balls as before and bake for a further 5 minutes. Then bake with the filling for about 25 minutes or whatever timings your recipe suggests.

I attended a very amusing and interesting cooking demonstration by a top New Zealand chef and we were given a huge lunch with lots of different local wines to try with each course. Ricotta featured in some of the recipes and he said how simple it is to make so I made some as soon as I got home. It is much cheaper and more delicious than shop-bought ricotta. I have used it in lots of recipes and my family love it with fresh peaches or a mound of berries for breakfast.

I make two quantities at the same time but I don't double the quantities as I love the fact that the recipe is so quick and easy to make this way.

Makes 500ml/2 cups
Wheat, gluten and
can be lactose-free

My Ricotta *Cheese*

750ml/3 cups full fat lactose-free milk or goat's/sheep's milk

375ml/1½ cups lactose-free or goat's double cream

½ teaspoon fine sea salt

3–4 tablespoons lemon juice, depending on how sour the lemons are

You will need a muslin, cheese cloth or old linen napkin to drain the cheese.

Combine the milk, cream and salt in a pan. Bring it to the boil but don't burn the base. Remove the pan from the heat and stir in the lemon juice. Leave for 20 minutes to curdle.

Line a large sieve or a colander with the chosen linen and place it over a bowl.

Pour the cream mixture into it and leave the whey to strain for about 30 minutes.

Discard the whey or use it in a traditional bread recipe.

You can use the ricotta immediately but it is better to chill it overnight in the fridge.

Tip: the longer you leave cheese to strain, the dryer it will become. I let it drain until the whey starts becoming slightly milky and then I know that it is perfect and creamy for us and the recipes.

Stockists & Useful Addresses

I hope that you will log on to my website www.antoinettesavill.com where you will find all sorts of recommendations and other useful information. I enjoy using Twitter and blogging, so please do log on and join in. www.twitter.com/A_savill

UNITED KINGDOM

Coeliac UK
3rd Floor
Apollo Centre
Desborough Road
High Wycombe
Bucks
HP11 2QW
Helpline: 0845 305 2060
Switchboard: 01494 437278
Opening hours: Mon-Fri, 9am–5pm

Scottish office
1 Saint Colme Street
Edinburgh
EH3 6AA
Tel: 0131 220 8342

Welsh office
Baltic House
Mount Stuart Square
Cardiff Bay
Cardiff
CF10 5FH
Tel: 0292 049 9732

Wellfoods Ltd
I still have not yet found a white bread or bread rolls as good as these, they freeze beautifully whether in slices or whole. The bread is good enough to be used for bread and butter pudding, queen of puddings, treacle tart and bread sauce. I freeze the crumbs in little bags and use them as I need them.

Antoinette Savill Signature Series Standard white loaf and pack of 4 white bread rolls.

Available mail order at:
Wellfoods Ltd
Towngate,
Mapplewell,
Barnsley,
South Yorkshire
S75 6AS
www.wellfoods.co.uk

Arla Lactofree
My favourite hard cheddar-style cheese and soft cream-style cheese is available in most large supermarkets and health food shops. Their cream is fabulous and whips perfectly, their milk and yogurt works and tastes like normal full fat dairy milk but everything is lactose-free.
www.lactofree.co.uk

Pure Products
Pure sunflower spread and soya soft and creamy (cream-cheese style) spread and are free from dairy and GM ingredients and suitable for vegetarians and vegans. I use them in all my recipes when I am cooking in Herefordshire. Their Soya spread is very good too but I prefer the taste and texture of sunflower.
www.puredairyfree.co.uk

Alpro Soya

Alpro soya is still the best single cream that I use in my recipes, for serving with fruit and other puddings, even making a wicked smoothie or savoury sauces and fillings for pies and quiches.

Alpro soya single cream 250ml is a useful size for the recipes. I also use their milk in everything but choose to work with the unsweetened chilled variety rather than the longer life ones.
www.alpro.com

Doves Farm Foods Ltd

This was established in 1978 and now you can buy their fabulous speciality flours almost anywhere. It is produced in a UK flour mill and most of the flour is organic. Doves Farm Gluten and Wheat Free Plain White Flour Blend and Doves Farm Gluten and Wheat Free Self Raising White Flour Blend are what I use in all the recipes if I am not using my own blend. They have never failed me and the flour is easily available in supermarkets, health food shops and on the mail order websites stocking allergy products.
www.dovesfarm.co.uk

Drossa Ltd

This is a very upmarket mail order collection of yummy gluten, wheat and some dairy-free foods. Wonderful gnocchi, tagliatelle and cannelloni, caper berries, mustards, Tzatziki Herb Mix and some very seductive macarons.
www.drossa.co.uk

St Helen's Farm

These are the best goat's products that I have tasted and have a lovely white and creamy look about them. Their cream is excellent as you can whip it, pour it and cook with it. The butter is so good that it is barely distinguishable from cows' butter and reacts in the same way in cooking too. The natural yogurt and cheeses are also mild and creamy and have worked perfectly in each recipe.
www.sthelensfarm.co.uk

Kinnerton Ltd

This is great chocolate for dairy, gluten and wheat-free cooking and I use it in all my recipes. Children like it for birthday cakes, cupcakes and chocolate sauce as it has a mild flavour. Kinnerton also make lots of novelty chocolates which are fun for Christmas, Easter and Halloween and useful as cake decorations too. I loved the advent calendars, lollipops and chocolate buttons.
www.kinnerton.com

NEW ZEALAND

Totally Gluten Free Bakery Ltd

The bakery is as its name suggests a dedicated gluten-free bakery with some delicious breads, cakes, scones, bagels, panini, tortilla, pizza bases and cookies. They have some dairy-free and also egg-free as well. You can order breads to be delivered anywhere in New Zealand. I loved their twisted cheese bread and their garlic and herb bread, served hot and golden.
www.glutenfreebakery.co.nz

Pasta D'Oro, South Island Fresh Foods Limited

Pasta d'Oro is a manufacturer and wholesaler of traditional Italian pasta products. Established since 1987 in Dunedin supplying mainly the food service industry nationwide with a range

of artisan pasta products. A selected range of products is also available through some supermarkets, shops and delis. Traditional methods and recipes that retain the freshness and goodness of the ingredients. Gluten, wheat and egg-free options. Supplied in 1kg bags, free-flow frozen potato gnocchi, dried penne, fusilli, fresh fettuccine and lasagne sheets.
www.pastadoro.co.nz

Piko Wholefoods
The Piko store has a huge choice of suitable flours and products for gluten, wheat and dairy-free cooking. They have a large range of products for all allergies and they are well known for their certified organic and GE-free products as well as being sensitive to local produce and Fairtrade. Good website and deliver around South Island.
www.pikowholefoods.co.nz

The Coeliac Society New Zealand
For help and advice on all aspects of gluten-free diet, you can contact them by email. They have a good site with lots of helpful information. You can shop from the website and they also advertise the well-respected Gluten-Free Food and Allergy Show dates. You can become a member.
www.coeliac.co.nz and www.coeliac.org.nz

AUSTRALIA

Australia has an excellent network of help for coeliacs which works for each state as the area is so huge. They helpfully list restaurants around Australia which is great for holidays, work visits and for the residents of course. The site has questions which experts answer, news and stories. There is a helpline.
www.coeliac.org.au

Gluten-Free Travel
Is an Australian travel agency specialising in travel arrangements for coeliacs. Their website contains lots of useful information as well as a list of all the coeliac societies round the world.
www.glutenfreetravel.com.au

UNITED STATES OF AMERICA

Celiac Support Association (CSA)
www.csaceliacs.org

Celiac Disease Foundation
www.celiac.org

Select Wisely
This is a really useful site in the USA. They make cards in different languages for all sorts of allergies so you can travel safely. There is international shipping and email delivery available for airport security letters.
www.selectwisely.com

CANADA

Canadian Celiac Association
www.celiac.ca/

Index

Also Available

LEARN TO COOK WHEAT, GLUTEN AND DAIRY FREE

100 step-by-step recipes

Antoinette Savill

Learn to Cook Wheat, Gluten and Dairy Free
Antoinette Savill

£14.99 Paperback
www.grubstreet.co.uk